D0298452

UK price
£5.95

AN ILLUSTRATED GUIDE TO

MODERN
FIGHTERS
AND ATTACK AIRCRAFT

Published by Salamander Books Limited
LONDON ● NEW YORK

AN ILLUSTRATED GUIDE TO

MODER FIGHTERS

AND ATTACK AIRCRAFT

Revised and updated edition featuring 20 new aircraft

Bill Gunston

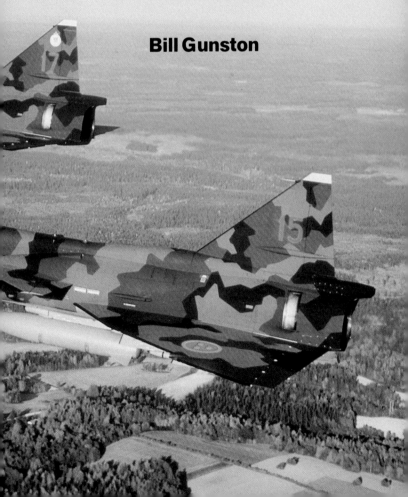

A Salamander Book

ISBN 0 86101 320 4

Distributed in the United Kingdom by
Hodder & Stoughton Services,
P.O. Box 6,
Mill Road,
Dunton Green,
Sevenoaks,
Kent TN13 2XX.

Contents

Credits

Author: Bill Gunston, former Technical Editor of *Flight International*, Compiler of *Jane's All the World's Aircraft* and contributor to many Salamander illustrated reference books.

Editor: Roger Chesneau
Designed by Little Oak Studios
Artwork: ©Salamander Books Ltd and ©Pilot Press Ltd, and by David Palmer and Stephen Seymour

Typeset: The Old Mill, London
Printed in Belgium by Proost International Book Production, Turnhout
Photographs: The publishers wish to thank the official government departments, the aircraft manufacturers and the individuals who have supplied photographs reproduced in this book

Aeritalia/Aermacchi/ EMBRAER AMX

Origin: Joint programme by Aeritalia Combat Aircraft Group and Aermacchi SpA of Italy, and EMBRAER of Brazil.
Type: Tactical attack and reconnaissance aircraft.
Engine: One 11,030lb (5,003kg) Rolls-Royce Spey 807 turbofan, produced in Italy under licence by Fiat, Piaggio and Alfa Romeo.
Dimensions: Span (over AAMs), 32ft 9¾in (10.0m); length 44ft 6½in (13.575m); height 15ft 0¾in (4.576m); wing area 226ft² (21m²).
Weights: Empty 13,228lb (6,000kg); max loaded 25,353lb (11,500kg).
Performance: Max speed with full external mission load at sea level 722mph (1,162km/h, Mach 0.95); cruising speed in bracket Mach 0.75 to 0.8; take-off run at max weight 3,120ft (950m); attack radius with 5min combat and 10 per cent reserves with 6,000lb (2,722kg) of external ordnance (hi-lo-hi) 320 miles (570km), (lo-lo-lo) 230 miles (370km).
Armament: Total external load of 7,716lb (3,500kg) carried on centreline pylon, four underwing pylons and AAM wingtip rails; internal gun(s) (Italy) one 20mm M61A-1 with 350 rounds, (Brazil) two 30mm DEFA 5-54 with 125 rounds each.
History: Start of design studies 1977; start of bilateral development January 1981; first flight (Italy) 1984, (Brazil) 1985.
Users: Brazil, Italy.

This machine's designation stems from Aeritalia/Macchi Xperimental, and it was started in 1977 as an Italian study project for a replacement for the G.91 and F-104G. The eminently sensible decision was taken to aim at a subsonic limiting Mach number, the result being an aircraft that promises to be light, compact, relatively cheap, possessed of good short-field performance, versatile in operation and capable of carrying a wide assortment of equipment

and weapons. In some respects it resembles a modernized Hunter, though of course it represents a different level of technology in aerodynamics, structure and systems. The participation of the Brazilian partner has not only broadened the market and manufacturing base but also expanded the variety of equipment and weapon fits.

The AMX will be used chiefly in tactical roles such as close air support and battlefield interdiction, operating with full fuel and weapons from unpaved strips less than 3,280ft (1,000m) in length. The design has attempted to maximize reliability and the ability to withstand battle damage, and to an exceptional extent everything on board is modular and quickly replaceable. The seat is a Martin-Baker 10L, fuel is divided between the fuselage and integral wings, and flight controls are dual hydraulic with manual back-up.

The two original customers have specified a simple range-only radar derived in Italy from the Israeli Elta M-2001. The Italian aircraft, of which 187 are planned to be delivered to the AMI to equip eight squadrons, will have a high standard of avionics, with a HUD (head-up display), INS and tacan, digital data highways and processing, an advanced cockpit display and a very comprehensive ECM installation. Any of three different photo-recon modules can be installed in a large bay in the lower right side of the fuselage, while an external IR/optronics recon pod can be carried on the centreline pylon. The Brazilian FAB expects to acquire 79 aircraft, with VOR/ILS but no INS, different guns and other avionics variations. The original FAB force requirement was for 144, and it is possible that this may be restored.

An unusual feature of the AMX is that it has no direct competitor, other than refurbished, second-hand A-7 Corsair IIs. The first prototype crashed, but the next five flew with complete success. Deliveries of production aircraft were to begin in late 1986. Meanwhile, the partners have privately developed a tandem two-seat version for training and tactical missions.

Below: Very few changes have proved necessary as a result of AMX flight testing. This prototype has dummy AAMs on the wing tips. The two-seat version will also have full weapons capability.

Atlas Aircraft Cheetah

Origin: Atlas Aircraft Corporation of South Africa (Pty) Ltd modification of Dassault-Breguet aircraft, assisted by Israel Aircraft Industries.

Type: Single-seat or two-seat interceptor, tactical strike aircraft, reconnaissance aircraft or trainer (depending on original Mirage sub-type).

Engine: One 15,873lb (7,200kg) thrust (max afterburner) SNECMA Atar 9K-50 turbojet, overhauled and part-manufactured by Atlas Aircraft.

Dimensions: Span 27ft (8.22m); length 53ft 11½in (16.45m); height 13ft 11¼in (4.25m); wing area 375ft² (34.84m²); foreplane area, probably similar to Kfir.

Weights: Empty (Cheetah D2Z) about 14,500lb (6,577kg), (E2Z) about 15,900lb (7,212kg); loaded (both) about 29,500lb (13,381kg).

Performance: Not disclosed, but claimed to be superior to that of any Atar-powered delta Mirage, apart from max speed and range which are unlikely to be significantly changed.

Armament: It has been claimed that the Cheetah carries 'only South African-made weapons'; these include two Armscor-made DEFA 5-52 guns each of 30mm calibre and with 125 rounds; two or four Armscor V3B Kukri dogfight AAMs; up to about 8,820lb (4,000kg) of bombs, rockets, cluster dispensers or other stores on seven external pylons.

History: Not disclosed, but original request dated 1982; ceremonial roll-out July 1986.

User: South Africa.

In about 1982 Atlas Aircraft was requested by the South African Defence Force to study the refurbishment and upgrading of its still-substantial force of Mirage IIICZ fighters, 16 of which were delivered from France in 1963–64 followed later by a further 24. The SAAF also received the IIIBZ and IIIDZ tandem trainers, the IIIEZ attack version and the upgraded IIIR2Z reconnaissance aircraft. The study, probably carried out with the assistance of Israel Aircraft Industries, threw up no major problem. The obvious thing to do was to copy as far as possible IAI's development of the Atar-engined Nesher, and some of the proven features of the Kfir (*qv*) apart from the latter's J79 engine.

Few details have been made available, but in mid-July 1986 the first of the rebuilt Mirages, named Cheetah, was ceremonially unveiled by President Botha. It was a rebuild of a two-seat Mirage IIID2Z, one of the later deliveries from Dassault and, as denoted by the '2' in the designation, fitted with the uprated 9K-50 engine. Almost all the features have been seen before on the

Below: In this view the almost total similarity to the IAI Kfir TC2 is apparent, including the ventral fin. The engine, however, remains an Atar. The insignia on the fin is a rampant lion.

Israeli aircraft. Modifications include the fitting of large fixed canard foreplanes high on the sides of the inlet ducts; the installation of a new multimode radar; the fitting of new wing leading edges, with prominent outboard drooping extensions and — not seen on any Mirage, which uses sawcuts — small fences inboard of the large dogtooth discontinuity; the addition of the same undernose instrumentation probe as on the Kfir TC2; and the addition of the same aircraft's undernose sensor and curved body fences low along the fuselage ahead of the inlets.

The main navigation and attack avionics are completely new. The radar is almost certainly the Israeli Elta EL/M-2021, a substantial multimode set much more capable than the small EL/M-2001B fitted to many Kfirs. Like the two-seat Kfir TC2, the complete radar nose is tilted downwards, with a kink on the underside in line with the windscreen. Several other Israeli avionics systems are fitted, as well as an unknown type of chaff/flare dispenser.

The intention is gradually to bring all SAAF delta Mirages up to the same high standard, fitting them for an extended service life and with considerably enhanced fighting capability. Priority is surely being given to upgrading the IIICZ fighters; other versions will probably follow. Atlas has said, 'About half of each aircraft is reconstructed. The programme includes new performance levels, and the replacement of many structural components and upgrading of flight systems'.

Below: The small wing fences are not on the Kfir TC2, and Cheetah's outboard leading-edge droops also appear to be more powerful.
All markings and insignia are of the modern low-contrast type.

BAe Buccaneer

Origin: British Aerospace, UK.
Type: Two-seat attack and reconnaissance aircraft.
Engines: Two 11,030lb (5,003kg) Rolls-Royce Spey 101 turbofans.
Dimensions: Span 44ft (13.41m); length 63ft 5in (19.33m). height 16ft 3in (4.95); wing area 514.7ft² (47.82m²).
Weights: Empty about 30,000lb (13,610kg); max loaded 62,000lb (28,123kg).
Performance: Max speed 690mph (1,110km/h) at sea level. range on typical hi-lo-hi strike mission with weapon load 2,300 miles (3,700km).
Armament: Rotating bomb door carries four 1,000lb (454kg) bombs or multisensor reconnaissance pack or 440gal tank; four wing pylons each stressed to 3,000lb (1,361kg), compatible with very wide range of guided and/or free-fall missiles. Total internal and external stores load 16,000lb (7,257kg).
History: First flight (NA.39) 30 April 1958, (production S.1) 23 January 1962, (prototype S.2) 17 May 1963, (production S.2) 5 June 1964; final delivery late 1975.
Users: South Africa, UK (RAF).

Below: After years of bitter opposition the RAF finally took the 'Bucc' because everything else was denied it. It then discovered the superb qualities of this great aircraft, and its crews have felt nothing could replace it. Here are 237 OCU and 208 Sqn S.2Bs.

In April 1957 the Defence White Paper proclaimed manned combat aircraft to be obsolete. Subsequently the Blackburn B.103, built to meet naval attack specification NA.39, was the only new British military aircraft that was not cancelled. Designed for carrier operation, its wing and tail were dramatically reduced in size as a result of powerful tip-to-tip boundary-layer control achieved by blasting hot compressed air bled from the engines from narrow slits. The S.1 (strike Mk 1) was marginal on power, but the greatly improved S.2 was a reliable and formidable aircraft.

The first 84 were ordered by the Royal Navy, but when the government ordered the phase-out of Britain's conventional carrier force, most were transferred to RAF Strike Command, designated S.2B when converted to launch Martel missiles. The RAF signed in 1968 for 43 new S.2Bs with new avionics and a refuelling probe.

Within the limits of crippling budgets the RAF Buccaneers have been updated by a few improved avionics, and have gradually been recognized as among the world's best long-range interdiction aircraft. When carrying a 4,000lb (1,814kg) bomb load a 'Bucc' at full power is faster than a Mirage, Phantom or F-16 at low level, and burns less fuel per mile. Many Red Flag exercises have demonstrated that a well-flown example is among the most difficult of all today's aircraft to shoot down.

In February 1985 British Aerospace was appointed prime contractor in a major update programme to fit surviving aircraft — slightly depleted to 60 following a wing fatigue problem — for a further long period of service. Nos 12 and 208 Sqns RAF at Lossiemouth are tasked in the maritime role, carrying Sea Eagle cruise missiles. Ferranti has updated the radar and fitted an inertial navigation system, while Marconi is updating the electronic-warfare suite.

BAe Harrier

Origin: British Aerospace, UK.
Type: Single-seat STOVL tactical attack and reconnaissance aircraft; (T.4) dual trainer or special mission aircraft.
Engine: One 21,500lb (9,752kg) thrust Rolls-Royce Pegasus 103 vectored-thrust turbofan.
Dimensions: Span 25ft 3in (7.7m), (with bolt-on tips) 29ft 8in; length (GR.3) 47ft 2in (14.38m), (T.4) 57ft 3in (17.45m); height (GR.3) 11ft 3in (3.43m); (T.4) 13ft 8in (4.17m); wing area 201.1ft² (18.68m²).
Weights: Empty (GR.3) 12,200lb (5,533kg), (T.4) 13,600lb (6,168kg); max (non-VTOL) 25,200lb (11,430kg).
Performance: Max speed over 737mph (1,186km/h, Mach 0.972) at low level; max dive Mach number 1.3; initial climb rate (VTOL weight) 50,000ft (15,240m)/min; service ceiling, over 50,000ft (15,240m); tactical radius on strike mission without drop tanks (hi-lo-hi) 260 miles (418km); ferry range 2,070 miles (3,300km).
Armament: All external, with many options. Underfuselage strakes each replaceable by pod containing one 30mm Aden or similar gun, with 150 rounds. Five or seven stores pylons, centre and two inboard each rated at 2,000lb (907kg), outers at 650lb (295kg) and tips (if used) at 220lb (100kg) for Sidewinder AAMs (first fitted during the Falklands crisis). Normal load 5,300lb (2,400kg), but 8,000lb (3,630kg) has been flown.
History: First hover (P.1127) 21 October 1960; (development Harrier) 31 August 1966; (Harrier GR.1) 28 December 1967; (T.2) 24 April 1969; squadron service (GR.1) 1 April 1969. GR.1 and T.2 now updated to GR.3 and T.4.
User: UK (RAF), USA (Marine Corps), Spain (Navy).

Below: A brace of GR.3s from 233 OCU, the RAF STOVL training unit, based at Wittering. This is also training pilots of the new GR.5.

Above: A GR.3 of No 4 Sqn RAF under a hide during exercises in West Germany. Hidden airpower might survive indefinitely in wartime.

Until May 1982 the Harrier was generally regarded (except by those familiar with it) as a quaint toy of an experimental nature. Since then it has become a battle-proven weapon in sustained intensive operations in conditions which would have kept other aircraft grounded. The Harrier, basically a machine of classic simplicity, pioneered the entire concept of STOVL (short take-off, vertical landing) combat operations, and the sustained mounting of close-support and reconnaissance missions from dispersed sites.

Though the Harrier is small it has a better range and weapon load than a Hunter, and it has also emerged as an air-combat adversary of extreme difficulty. Though not designed as a fighter, its combination of small size, unusual shape, lack of visible smoke and unique agility conferred by the ability to vector the engine thrust direction (to make 'impossible' square turns, violent deceleration or unexpected vertical movements without change of attitude) make even the original Harrier a most unpopular opponent for any modern interceptor.

The RAF Harrier GR.3 has an inertial nav/attack system, laser ranger and marked-target seeker and fin-mounted passive warning receivers; it is planned to install internal ECM. RAF Germany has two squadrons (Nos 3 and 4) at Gutersloh, while No 1 Sqn and No 233 OCU are at Wittering.

A total of 102 Harriers were sold to the US Marine Corps, which designates the aircraft AV-8A or (following an update programme) AV-8C. These aircraft are simplified, the inertial navigation system being removed and various other avionics changes being made, including replacement of the Martin-Baker seat by the Stencel S-III. The Marine Corps aircraft are not normally used for sustained low-level operations but only for dive bombing and basic attack missions. Similar aircraft are used by the Spanish Navy, which calls them VA-1 Matadors. There is also a tandem dual-control trainer, called Harrier T.4 by the RAF, TAV-8A by the USMC, and VAE-1 by the Spanish Navy.

BAe Hawk

Origin: British Aerospace, UK.
Type: Trainer, light interceptor and light attack aircraft.
Engine: One Rolls-Royce Turboméca Adour turbofan, (T.1) 5,200lb (2,359kg) Mk 151, (50−53 and T-45A) 5,340lb (2,422kg) Mk 851, (Mk 60 onwards) 5,700lb (2,586kg) Mk 860, (Hawk 200) 5,850lb (2,654kg) Adour 871.
Dimensions: Span 30ft 10in (9.4m); length (over probe) 39ft 2½in (11.95m), (200) 36ft 1in (11.0m); height 13ft 5in (4.09m); wing area 179.54ft² (16.69m²).
Weights: Empty 7,450lb (3,379kg); loaded (trainer, clean) 12,000lb (5,443kg), (attack mission) 16,260lb (7,375kg).
Performance: Max speed 630mph (1,014km/h) at low level; Mach number in shallow dive 1.2; initial climb rate 6,000ft (1,830m)/min, (200) 11,510ft (3,508m)/min; service ceiling 50,000ft (15,240m); range on internal fuel 750 miles (1,207km), (200, two drop tanks) 2,237 miles (3,600km).
Armament: Three or five hard-points (two outboard optional) each rated at 1,000lb (454kg), (export Hawk) 6,800lb (3,085kg) weapon load; centreline point normally equipped with 30mm gun pod and ammunition; intercept role, two AIM-9L Sidewinder; (200) increased load options and one or two Aden 25mm or 30mm or Mauser 27mm guns mounted internally.
History: First flight 21 August 1974; service delivery 1976.
Users: Abu Dhabi, Algeria, Dubai, Finland, Indonesia, Kenya, Kuwait, Saudi Arabia, Switzerland, UK (RAF), USA (Navy), Zimbabwe.

Though this is the only new all-British military aircraft for 15 years, the Hawk serves as a model of the speed and success that can be achieved when an experienced team is allowed to get on with the job. The RAF ordered 175 of these superb trainers, equipping No 4 FTS at Valley in the advanced pilot training role and also No 1 TWU (Tac Weapons Unit) at Brawdy, and No 2 TWU at Chivenor, in the weapons training role.

RAF Hawks have the lowest accident record for any known military jet in history, and defect rates are cut by 70 per cent whilst halving maintenance man-hours per flight hour. Despite the aircraft's greater size and power, fuel burn has been dramatically reduced compared with the Gnat. Hawks also equip the *Red Arrows* aerobatic display team.

In 1981 it was announced that, to back up RAF Strike Command's very limited fighter defence forces, about 90 Hawks would be equipped to fire AIM-9L Sidewinders in the light interception role. Under current planning about 72 are actually armed with the missiles.

Below: This T.1 bears the crossed sword and torch badge of No 1 Tactical Weapons Unit RAF, but not a squadron marking. It is carrying a 30mm Aden gun and practice bomb racks under the wings.

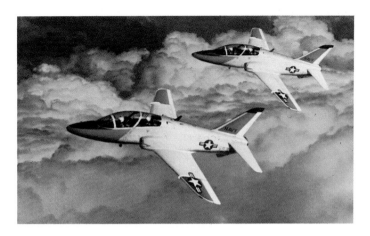

Above: Though very much a Hawk, the T-45A Goshawk is totally rede-signed in detail to meet the contrasting needs of the USN. Weapons delivery capability will be provided, but the Navy may not use it.

In addition the Hawk was selected in 1981 as the undergraduate pilot trainer of the US Navy, as the T-45A Goshawk, with full carrier equipment and major airframe changes including a nose gear with two wheels strengthened for nose-tow catapulting, two side airbrakes instead of one belly speed brake, and various items in carbon-fibre composites. Up to 300 are being supplied from 1987, the prime contractor being McDonnell Douglas.

Most of the export customers other than the US Navy use their Hawks in at least a weapons training role, and some task them with combat missions. BAe is marketing a Series 100 dedicated attack version of the Hawk with digital avionics, inertial navigation, optional laser ranging, HUDs in both cockpits and various features based on the F-16A.

In 1985 BAe took the decision to build a prototype of a dedicated single-seat version, tailored to air combat, attack, reconnaissance and virtually all other tactical roles. This began a very successful flight development programme in May 1986 but, sadly, it was flown into the ground during a demonstration in July 1986. There was never any suggestion of a fault in the aircraft, and it is probable that many Hawk 200s will be built in the next 20 years. It offers customers an outstandingly effective multirole aircraft needing no develop-ment — and one at an extremely competitive price.

Below: The BAe Hawk 200 will be a major programme, with customers from many countries. The main nose sensor can be a multimode radar, or alternatively a FLIR or a laser.

BAe Sea Harrier

Origin: British Aerospace, UK.
Type: Multirole STOVL naval combat aircraft.
Engine: One 21,500lb (9,752kg) thrust Rolls-Royce Pegasus 104 vectored-thrust turbofan.
Dimensions: Span 25ft 3in (7.7m); length 47ft 7in (14.5m); height 12ft 2in (3.71m); wing area 201.1ft² (18.68m²).
Weights: Empty, not disclosed but about 12,250lb (5,557kg); max (non-VTOL) 26,200lb (11,880kg).
Performance: Max speed over 737mph (1,186km/h); typical lo attack speed 690mph (1,110km/h); hi intercept radius (3min combat plus reserves and vertical landing) 460 miles (750km); lo strike radius 288 miles (463km).
Armament: Normally two 30mm Aden Mk 4 each with 150 rounds; five hardpoints for max weapon load of 8,000lb (3,630kg) including Sea Eagle or Harpoon ASMs, Sidewinder AAMs and very wide range of other stores.
History: First flight 20 August 1978; service delivery 18 June 1979; first squadron commissioned 19 September 1979.
Users: India (Navy), UK (RN).

Above: This FRS.1 is being flown from Yeovilton by Lt Cdr Rod Frederickson, CO of 800 NAS. Apart from tanks it is carrying a training Sidewinder (not actually fired) on the left outer pylon. STMs (Sidewinder Training Missiles) simulate the electronics of the actual missile as it locks-on to an airborne target.

Right: A Sea Harrier FRS.1 venting fuel from the wing-mounted jettison pipes. The twin blade aerials behind the cockpit serve the UHF homing radio, while the rectangular holes further aft are the inlet and exhaust for the gas-turbine APU (auxiliary power unit) which renders the aircraft independent of ground power or starting supplies. The red stripes on top of the fuselage indicate engine access panelling, a 'no step' area.

After years of delay caused by various kinds of disbelief and indecision the Sea Harrier at last got the go-ahead in May 1975, though even then the idea of sea-going fixed-wing airpower was still as taboo as RAF combat aircraft had been at the start of the Harrier programme. Gradually the proposed 'through-deck-cruiser' became openly spoken of as a carrier for this STOVL aircraft which was most successfully developed from the Harrier chiefly by redesigning the forward fuselage. The deeper structure provides for a versatile and compact Ferranti Blue Fox radar, which folds 180° for shipboard stowage, and a new cockpit with the seat raised to provide space for a much-enhanced nav/at-tack/combat system and to give an all-round view.

The Royal Navy purchased 24, plus a further 10, FRS.1s, the designation meaning 'fighter reconnaissance strike' (strike normally means nuclear, but the Fleet Air Arm has not confirmed this capability). In the NATO context the main task is air defence at all altitudes, normally with direction from surface vessels, either as DLI (deck-launched intercept) or CAP (combat air patrol).

In the Falklands fighting, in which almost all the RN Sea Harriers (28 out of 32) took part, these aircraft repeatedly demonstrated their ability to fly six sorties a day in extremely severe weather, with maintenance by torchlight at night often in hail blizzards. Serviceability was consistently around 95 per cent each morning. CAPs were flown at 10,000ft (3,000m) at 290mph (463km/h) and within a few seconds it was possible to be closing on an enemy at 690mph (1,100km/h) just above the sea; 24 Argentine aircraft were claimed by AIM-9L Sidewinders and seven by guns. In air-to-ground missions the main stores were 1,000lb (454kg) bombs, Paveway 'smart' bombs and BL.755 clusters. Many new techniques were demonstrated, including 4,000-mile (6,440km) flights to land on ships (sometimes by pilots who had never landed on a ship), and operations from quickly added sheet laid on the top row of containers in a merchant ship.

From this harsh self-sufficient campaign it is a major step to the more sophisticated European environment of greater density and diversity of forces, and especially of emitters (though Sea Harriers did use jammer pods in the South Atlantic). Nearer to Europe, the Grumman E-2C and other aircraft would normally be available for direction, and the Sea Harrier is envisaged as filling the fleet defensive band between ship-to-air missiles and long-range F-14s with Phoenix AAMs. Its ESM fit is more advanced than that of land- ▶

▶ based Harriers, and is used as a primary aid to intercept emitting aircraft (or, it is expected, sea-skimming missiles). Pilots normally operate as individuals, flying any mission for which they are qualified.

By the middle of 1984 23 additional aircraft had been ordered to replace losses from all causes (6) and increase the establishment of the three combat squadrons, 800, 801 and 809 NAS — normally embarked aboard *Invincible, Illustrious* and *Hermes* (later *Ark Royal*) — and the training unit, 899 NAS, at Yeovilton.

Under a mid-life improvement programme, being implemented in 1986–90, the Royal Navy FRS.1 aircraft are to be updated to have a lookdown-shootdown capability with a new radar of pulse-doppler type, the Ferranti Blue Vixen. This will considerably upgrade all-round capability, and in particular will match the range of the new Sea Eagle anti-ship missile. It is ex-

pected that JTIDS (joint tactical information distribution system), a secure voice data-link, Zeus active ECM and Guardian radar warning will be installed, together with four AIM-120A (Amraam) AAMs, and the cockpit will be updated. The first of the rebuilt Sea Harrier FRS.2s was to fly in 1986.

The only export customer so far has been the Indian Navy. This service purchased six FRS.51s and two T.60 two-seat trainers, followed by a repeat order for ten Mk 51s and two trainers. They operate with No 300 Sqn from shore bases and from INS *Vikrant*. Orders for further aircraft have been announced, following the transfer of *Hermes* to the Indian Navy as INS *Virat*.

Below: An FRS.51 of No 300 (White Tiger) Squadron of the Indian Navy. These aircraft are almost identical to the FRS.1 except for a switch from liquid to gaseous oxygen, and Matra Magic missiles.

Dassault-Breguet Mirage III, 5, 50, IIING

Origin: Avions Marcel Dassault-Breguet Aviation, France (actual manufacture dispersed through French and Belgian industry).

Type: Single-seat or two-seat interceptor, tactical strike aircraft, trainer or reconnaissance aircraft (depending on sub-type).

Engine: (IIIC) One 13,225lb (6,000kg) thrust (max afterburner) SNECMA Atar 9B turbojet; (most other III and some 5) 13,670lb (6,200kg) Atar 9C; (IIIR2Z, NG and 50) 15,873lb (7,200kg) Atar 9K-50.

Dimensions: Span 27ft (8.22m); length (exc probe) (IIIC) 48ft 5in (14.75m), (IIIE) 49ft 3½in (15.03m), (5) 51ft 0¼in (15.55m); height 13ft 11½in (4.25m); wing area 375ft² (35.0m²).

Weights: Empty (IIIC) 13,570lb (6,156kg), (IIIE) 15,540lb (7,050kg), (IIIR) 14,550lb (6,600kg), (IIIB) 13,820lb (6,270kg), (5) 14,550lb (6,600kg); loaded (IIIC) 19,700lb (8,936kg), (IIIE, IIIR, 5) 29,760lb (13,500kg), (IIIB) 26,455lb (12,000kg).

Performance: Max speed (all models, clean) 870mph (1,400km/h, Mach 1.14) at sea level, 1,450mph (2,335km/h, Mach 2.2) at altitude; initial climb rate over 16,400ft (5,000m)/min, time to 36,090ft/11,000m, 3min; service ceiling (Mach 1.8) 55,775ft (17,000m); range (clean) at altitude about 1,000 miles (1,610km); combat radius in attack mission with two bombs and tanks (hi-altitude) 745 miles (1,200km); ferry range with three external tanks 2,485 miles (4,000km).

Armament: Two 30mm DEFA 5-52 cannon, each with 125 rounds (normally fitted to all versions except when IIIC carries rocket-boost pack); three 1,000lb (454kg) external pylons for bombs, missiles or tanks, (Mirage 5) seven external pylons with max capacity of 9,260lb (4,200kg).

History: First flight (prototype Mirage III-001) 17 November 1956, (production IIIC) 9 October 1960, (prototype 5) 19 May 1967, (Belgian-assembled 5BA) May 1970.

Users: (III) Abu Dhabi, Argentina, Australia, Brazil, Egypt, France, Israel, Lebanon, Libya, Pakistan, South Africa, Spain, Switzerland, Venezuela; (5) Abu Dhabi, Belgium, Colombia, Egypt, France, Gabon, Libya, Pakistan, Peru, Saudi Arabia, Venezuela, Zaïre; (50) Chile.

By far the most commercially successful fighter ever built in Western Europe, the tailless delta Mirage has had little local competition, but has had to contend in the world market with the F-104 and F-5. It had the advantage of proven combat success in 1967 with Israel, the first export customer, and this catapulted it into the limelight and brought about sales of 1,410 to 20 different air forces.

The initial Mirage IIIC, now being withdrawn from l'Armée de l'Air but still operating in South Africa, has an early Cyrano radar giving a limited all-weather and night interception capability. The original armament comprised the Matra R.530 missile, with an IR or radar homing head, and an alternative of two 30mm guns or a booster rocket pack, the tankage for which occupied the gun ammunition bay. This rocket is still available, but with the advent of more powerful Atar engines it has not been adopted by other customers.

Most of today's aircraft are variants either of the IIIE, a slightly lengthened fighter-bomber with better radar and more comprehensive navigation and weapon-delivery avionics, or the 5, a simplified model without radar and able to carry additional fuel or bombs within the same gross weight. This has appealed strongly to Third World countries because of its lower price, and if flown in good weather it has few serious limitations apart from the basic ones ▶

Above: A Belgian Mirage 5BA, one of the simplified Mirage 5 series. Such aircraft are of very limited use in Belgium, which suffers variable weather. The one thing their 5BA does have is the Loral Rapport II internal ECM system.

Left: A Mirage IIIB trainer of EC2 of the French Armée de l'Air. This version can carry weapons, but has no radar. The Mirage IIID version was assembled in Australia for the RAAF. The total number of two-seaters produced was 186, equipping twenty air forces.

▶ that afflict all early tailless deltas — the need for a long runway and the inability to make sustained tight turns without speed bleeding off rapidly. The Mirage III was, in fact, planned to have low-pressure tyres and to operate from rough strips, but the actual tyre pressure combined with the extremely high take-off and landing speeds make this a very rare occurrence.

Some customers have bought tandem dual trainers, others the IIIR with a camera-filled nose (South Africa's R2Z having the uprated 9K-50 engine, and several users the chin bulge showing the installation of advanced doppler). Chile bought the latest production model, the 50, and these have been updated with canards by Israel.

At the time of writing a customer has yet to emerge for the IIING (Nouvelle

Right: One of the batch of 16 Mirage 50s bought by the only customer for this version, Chile. Powered by the uprated 9K-50 engine, this model also has an inertial navigation system, HUD (head-up display) and several other features which bring this basically 30-year-old aircraft more up to date.

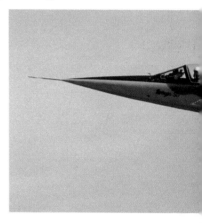

Below: Distinguished by its small fixed canards and leading-edge root extensions, the Mirage IIING (also written 3NG) first flew on 21 December 1982 but has so far not found a customer.

Génération) development which adds a fly-by-wire flight control system, wing-root strakes, fixed canards, inertial navigation, a HUD, Cyrano IV radar, a laser ranger and additional weapon stations to take advantage of the increased maximum weight of 32,400lb (14,700kg). Some customers, such as Peru, have updated their Mirages using Dassault-Breguet kits for a HUD, inertial navigation system, laser ranger and Magic AAMs, and the update market for Mirage deltas is now a major one.

The Mirage III/5 story is, however, far from over. In Switzerland and in France, canard foreplanes are being fitted to add more manoeuvrability in combat. A modification programme is underway on Swiss IIIs, while Dassault are hoping to attract orders for the latest IIING.

Dassault-Breguet Mirage F1

Origin: Avions Marcel Dassault-Breguet Aviation (France) in partnership with Aérospatiale, SABCA (Belgium) and CASA (Spain); licensed to Atlas Aircraft, South Africa.

Type: Single-seat multimission fighter; (E) all-weather strike aircraft; (R) reconnaissance aircraft; (B) dual trainer.

Engine: One 15,873lb (7,200kg) thrust (max afterburner) SNECMA Atar 9K-50 augmented turbojet.

Dimensions: Span 27ft 6¾in (8.4m); length (F1.C) 49ft 2½in (15.0m). (F1.E) 50ft 11in (15.53m); height (F.1C) 14ft 9in (4.5m), (F1.E) 14ft 10½in (4.56m); wing area 269.1ft² (25m²).

Weights: Empty (F1.C) 16,314lb (7,400kg), (F1.E) 17,857lb (8,100kg); loaded (clean) (F1.C) 24,030lb (10,900kg), (F1.E) 25,450lb (11,540kg); (max) (F1.C) 32,850lb (14,900kg), (F1.E) 33,510lb (15,200kg).

Performance: Max speed (clean F.1C/E) 910mph (1,470km/h, Mach 1.2) at sea level, 1,450mph (2,335km/h, Mach 2.2) at altitude; climb rate (sustained to Mach 2 at 33,000ft) (F1.C) 41,930–47,835ft (12,780-14,580m)/min; service ceiling (F1.C) 65,600ft (20,000m); range with max weapons (hi-lo-hi) (F1.C) 560 miles (900km), (F1.E) 621 miles (1,000km); ferry range (F1.C) 2,050 miles (3,300km).

Armament: (Both versions) Two 30mm DEFA 5-53 cannon, each with 135 rounds; five pylons, rated at 4,500lb (2,000kg) on centreline, 2,800lb (1,350kg) inners and 1,100lb (500kg) outers; launch rails on tips rated at 280lb (120kg) for AAMs; total weapon load 8,820lb (4,000kg). Typical air combat weapons, two Matra 550 Magic for close combat, one/two Matra Super 530 for long-range homing. Optional reconnaissance pod containing cameras, SAT Cyclope infrared linescan and EMI side-looking radar.

History: First flight (F1-01) 23 December 1966, (production F1.C) 15 February 1973, (F1.B trainer) 26 May 1976; service delivery (F1.C) 14 March 1973, (F1.R) 7 September 1983.

Users: Ecuador, France, Greece, Iraq, Jordan, Kuwait, Libya, Morocco, Qatar, South Africa, Spain.

►

Above: Seen here in service with EC 2/5 Ile de France of l'Armée de l'Air, the F1.C-200 is equipped with a fixed flight-refuelling probe, no provision for a folding probe having been incorporated. Under the fuselage is a big 484gal (2,200l) drop tank.

Below: South Africa and Libya, proscribed by most arms exporters, have been major customers for this F1.A version without multimode radar but specially configured for ground attack missions. This example, notable for extra chin avionics including a laser designator, is depicted carrying eight Durandal anti-runway weapons, each of which is first braked and then fired steeply downwards.

Above: This F1.C, serving with l'Armée de l'Air's EC12 wing, is fully armed for the air-to-air mission with Matra Magic dogfight missiles on the wing tips and Matra Super 530Fs under the wings.

▶ In the early 1960s Dassault thought the Mirage III would soon need replacing and studied various configurations before deciding on a high fixed wing of conventional form, plus a horizontal tail. The F1 has a wing much smaller than that of the deltas but so much more efficient that the aircraft has shorter field length, slower landing, and (with 40 per cent greater internal fuel) three times the supersonic endurance, or twice the tactical radius at low level, with superior all-round manoeuvrability. With long-stroke, twin-wheel main gears and a landing speed of 143mph (230km/h), the F1 is also more genuinely able to use short, unpaved airstrips.

L'Armée de l'Air achieved operational F.1C capability with 30e Escadre at Reims, followed by 5e Escadre at Orange — whose three squadrons include 25

of the F1.C-200 type with permanent FR probes to permit non-stop deployment to Djibouti, 3,100 miles, (5,000km) away, and similar distant points — and EC 12 at Cambrai.

Equipped with Cyrano IV radar and the excellent combination of Magic and Super 530 AAMs, the F1.C is one of the best interceptors in Western Europe, though its relatively small size and low power inevitably place it at a disadvantage in either the long-range patrol mission or close air combat.

All models have the uprated 9K-50 engine, and most customers have bought a comprehensive EW suite including the Thomson-CSF Type BF RWR. In a few air forces, including l'Armée de l'Air, the same supplier's Remora self-protection jammer pod is carried, and in the dedicated ECM role the usual jammer is the powerful Caiman. On the other hand, few customers have bothered about the very large increase in stand-off interception capability conferred by the Super 530F radar-guided AAM, even though this is a capability available from no other aircraft outside the two super-powers apart from the Viggen, the JA37 and the Tornado ADV. Most export customers have matched the F1 with the relatively cheap Magic dogfight AAM. In the second half of the decade the completely new Mle 30-791B gun will become available, firing higher-performance 30mm ammunition at 2,500rds/min.

There are four basic sub-variants of F1. Most have been derived from the F1.C with radar, and this family includes the F1.E multirole model with inertial navigation, a central computer and a HUD. The F1.A, used mainly by Libya and South Africa, is a simplified model with a slim, non-radar nose, configured mainly for ground attack; the F1.B tandem-seat dual-pilot model is a trainer with full combat capability but reduced fuel; and the F1.R is a dedicated reconnaissance version with cameras and other sensors.

Below: One of the largest export customers for the Mirage F1 series is Spain, with a total of 72 delivered. In the Ejercito del Aire (Spanish Air Force), the F1.CE is known as the C.14, and the F1.B and multirole F1.E are also in service. Since delivery flight-refuelling probes have been added and the weapon fit updated.

Dassault-Breguet Mirage 2000

Origin: Avions Marcel Dassault-Breguet Aviation, France; licensed to Egyptian Government factory, Helwan, and Hindustan Aeronautics Ltd, India.

Type Multirole fighter with emphasis on interception and air superiority combat.

Engine: One SNECMA M53-5 afterburning bypass turbojet (low-ratio turbofan) with max thrust of 12,350lb (5,602kg) dry and 19,840lb (9,000kg) with afterburner.

Dimensions: Span 29ft 6in (9.0m); length (2000) 47ft 1in (14.35m), (2000B) 47ft 9in (14.55m); height 17ft 6in (5.3m); wing area 441ft² (41m²).

Weights: Empty 16,315lb (7,400kg); normal take-off, air-intercept mission 33,000lb (14,969kg); max 36,375lb (16,500kg).

Performance: Max continuous speed at 36,000ft (11,000m) 1,320mph (2,124km/h, Mach 2.2); maximum attack speed at low level 690mph (1,110km/h); range (two tanks) over 1,118 miles (1,800km).

Armament: Two 30mm DEFA 5-53 cannon; normal air-intercept load two Matra Super 530 and two Matra 550 Magic AAMs; (2000N only) one ASMP nuclear cruise missile, able to carry a 150-kilotonne warhead up to 62 miles (100km).Intention is to develop ground-attack version with max overload of 13,225lb (6,000kg) of weapons and/or tanks and ECM pods on nine external hardpoints.

History: Announcement of project December 1975; first flight 10 March 1978; production delivery December 1983.

Users: Abu Dhabi, Egypt, France, Greece, India, Peru.

Superficially almost identical to earlier Mirage deltas, the 2000 is in fact a totally new aircraft, with dramatically enhanced capabilities. Very strongly biased to the air superiority mission, the 2000 was made possible only by the emergence of CCV (control configured vehicle) technology in the USA, which by combining FBW (fly-by-wire) signalling with instant-action computer control and multilane channel redundancy allows a fighter to be made basically unstable. A further great advantage over the Mirage III is that the wing has full-span leading-edge flaps which provide controlled camber for use in different flight regimes. For slow speeds and landing the fully drooped leading

edge allows the trailing-edge elevons to act as flaps, in contrast to the elevons of older Mirages which have to be deflected upwards, in effect greatly adding to weight, not lift.

The M53 engine is almost a turbojet, its bypass ratio being very low and the overall pressure ratio of only 9.3 showing the degree to which it is optimized to supersonic speed at very high altitude. Thus it is at a great disadvantage in fuel burn in the normal subsonic regime which accounts for more than 95 per cent of even a Mirage 2000's flight time.

Early Mirage 2000s were powered by the lower-rated M53-2 engine, but the production machines have the M53-5 as given in the specification. In 1985 deliveries began of the uprated M53-P2, with a peak afterburning thrust of 21,360lb (9,689kg), the first batch of which were fitted to the initial production 2000N aircraft. Some export customers have also specified the P2 engine.

In the attack mission the aircraft is further penalized by its large delta wing, which puts it very high in the 'unacceptable' regime in the plot of indicated airspeed at low level against the number of 0.5g bumps experienced per minute. This does not worry some customers, who see their Mirage 2000s purely as air-combat aircraft, in which rôle the combination of guns, Magic dogfight AAMs and radar-guided Super 530D AAMs promises to be a good one, though the 530D matched to the RDI pulse-doppler radar has yet to be exported and the radar itself has been seriously delayed. Thus the RDM radar, a simplified earlier set, is fitted to all current Mirage 2000s instead of only those for export.

The basic French fighter version is designated 2000C1 (*chasse*, single-seat). Deliveries began in 1983, and in July 1984 the first combat unit, Escadre de Chasse 1/2 Cigognes, became operational at Dijon with ten C1s and four tandem two-seat 2000B trainers. In 1985–86 EC 3/2 Alsace became operational at the same base, followed in 1987 by ECT (Escadre de Chasse Tactique) 2/2 Côte d'Or. More 2000C1s have been delivered during 1986. ▶

Below: An early-production Mirage 2000 of EC1/2 Cigognes at Dijon, which became operational in July 1984. Normal missile armament comprises two Super 530D radar-guided weapons inboard and two Magic IR-homing dogfight missiles. The planned RDI radar has been delayed, and all 2000s so far have the RDM radar (previously intended only for export customers). The only exception is the nuclear 2000N, which has the Antilope V terrain-following radar, plus considerably improved electronic countermeasures (ECM) and other changes; 85 examples of this version are expected to be in service by 1988.

▶ In addition, l'Armée de l'Air is receiving the first of a restressed and upgraded 2000N (*nucléaire*) attack version. First flown in 1983, this is a tandem two-seater stressed to fly at 690mph (1,110km/h) at low altitude whilst carrying an ASMP stand-off missile (see specification). The 2000N has an Antilope V terrain-following radar, two inertial platforms, a colour display in the cockpit and improved ECM. It was planned to have 36 of this version in service by 1988, the first recipients being units of the 4e Escadre at Luxeuil and the 7e at St Dizier. By the end of the 1988 defence programme, l'Armée de l'Air expects to have received 139 2000C1 fighters, 85 2000N nuclear delivery aircraft and 19 2000B trainers, and output by 1989 is expected to reach ten per month.

Dassault-Breguet has gained several important export contracts. Egypt has ordered 16 2000EMs and four two-seat BMs, all with the P2 engine. India expected to produce about 110 under licence after importing 40 (36 2000H and four 2000TH trainers, most with the Dash-5 engine), but Indian manufacture has been rejected. The IAF name is Vajra (Divine Thunderstreak), bestowed when No 225 Sqn at Gwalior received its first aircraft. Abu Dhabi has ordered 36 (22 EAD, six DAD trainers and eight of an RAD reconnaissance version with a multisensor external pod). Peru planned to order 26, but to save 'over $500 million' cut the order back to 12. Greece is buying 36 2000EG single-seaters and four 2000BG trainers.

Altogether the Mirage 2000 offers countries able to afford its high price an excellent small air-combat fighter, strongly biased towards high-altitude interception. It has a good spectrum of avionics and weapons, and well-conceived EW and ECM installations. Provision is made for a detachable inflight-refuelling probe above the right side of the nose.

Above: Prototypes of the Mirage 2000 and, further away, the big twin-engined Mirage 4000. The latter was built with Dassault money, first flying on 9 March 1979, but failed to find a customer.

Below. The 2000B tandem-seat trainer has an extended dorsal spine in which are accommodated some of the avionics displaced by the rear cockpit; guns also are omitted. This 2000B serves with EC1/2.

Dassault-Breguet Rafale

Origin: Avions Marcel Dassault-Breguet Aviation, France.
Type Experimental combat aircraft, to lead to future tactical and naval combat aircraft.
Engines: Two 16,000lb (7,258kg) thrust General Electric F404-400 augmented turbofans.
Dimensions: Span (over empty missile pylons) 36ft 9in (11.2m); length 51ft 10in (15.8m); height 17ft (5.18m); wing area 506ft² (47m²).
Weights: Empty equipped 20,940lb (9,500kg); combat weight (4 Mica and 2 Magic AAMs) 30,865lb (14,000kg); max loaded 44,090lb (20,000kg).
Performance: Max speed (clean, hi-altitude) 1,320mph (2,135km/h, Mach 2); (clean, sea level) 920mph (1,480km/h); take-off run (max weight) under 2,300ft (700m); combat radius (max weapons) 400 miles (644km).
Armament: One 30mm internal gun; pylons under centreline, air-inlet ducts, two under each wing and on wing tips for total attack load of up to 7,715lb (3,500kg). This load can comprise two LGBs (laser-guided bombs) or Armat anti-radar missiles or groups of Durandal or Belouga anti-runway weapons, two drop tanks, EO (electro-optical) and ECM (electronic countermeasures) pods, and up to six air-defence missiles (typically four Mica and two Magic).
History: Engineering go-ahead 1983; first flight 4 July 1986; operational service date 1996.
User: To be France.

Originally known as the ACX (Avion de Combat Expérimental), the Rafale (Squall) is the technology demonstrator intended to underpin the next generation of French combat aircraft. These comprise the ACT (Avion de Combat Tactique) for l'Armée de l'Air and the ACM (Avion de Combat Marin) for l'Aéronavale. The latter will be equipped for operation from the *Charles de Gaulle* class nuclear aircraft carriers.

Features of the Rafale include basically unstable design, with a rear cropped-delta wing and close-coupled canards, digital avionics with quadruply redundant FBW (fly-by-wire) flight controls, and an advanced cockpit with a Martin-Baker Mk 10 seat inclined back at 30–40°, a sidestick controller, a large holographic HUD, multifunction colour panel displays, and provision for fly-by-light fibre optical links and for speech-recognition, voice-activated pilot inputs.

The aircraft is made from many advanced materials. Most of the wings, foreplane and vertical tail are of carbon fibre, the wing root fairings and wing tips are of Kevlar, the air-inlet ducts are of aluminium-lithium alloy and the leading-edge drooping slats are of superplastic-formed titanium. Wing camber can naturally be varied under computer control throughout each flight to achieve the highest possible manoeuvrability with 'carefree' handling, the ▶

Below: In many ways, such as the aerodynamics and wing structure, the Rafale is less advanced and simpler than the rival EAP, and Dassault-Breguet also hope (despite developing land and carrier versions) to reduce the weight considerably. Engines are American GE F404s, pending availability of the new French M88.

▶ pilot never being able to overstress the structure nor approach dangerous conditions near the edge of the flight envelope. The inlets, one for each engine, are plain, sharp-lipped entries without variable geometry, but their location under the outward-spreading portions of the V-section fuselage gives excellent inlet behaviour at extreme angles of attack.

The landing gears are by Messier-Hispano-Bugatti. The steerable twin-wheel nose unit retracts forwards under the cockpit, while the single main wheels retract forwards to like flat under the air-inlet trunks. Michelin radial tyres are fitted, and all three units have carbon/carbon brakes with fly-by-wire control. Production aircraft will probably have both a braking parachute and an arrester hook.

Above: The prototype Rafale seen after completion but in intermediate primer paint which serves merely to disguise the materials used. The latter included carbon fibre (much of the wing and tail), Kevlar (root fairings and nose) and superplastic titanium (leading-edge slats). Messier-Hispano-Bugatti supplied the landing gears, all of which have carbon/carbon brakes and FBW control and retract forwards.

Right: Compared with the EAP the prototype Rafale has a simpler and smaller wing with prominent fairings over the four elevon power units. BAe also rejected tip-mounted missiles on the score of high drag; at present the Rafale carries Magic AAMs in this location.

Flight control is exercised by three sections of elevon on each wing, operated differentially or symmetrically, the foreplanes, and the single large rudder, all operated by hydraulic power units with an FBW control system. The slats, already mentioned, are computer controlled to operate with the elevons to enhance lift at high angles of attack. Twin airbrakes are mounted above the shallow but broad fuselage beside the ram-air cooling inlet in the front of the dorsal fin. Eventually it is expected that the Rafale will be fitted with radar and other combat equipment.

Flight testing has been proceeding successfully throughout the second half of 1986. Serge Dassault said in July 1986 that, though the programme was conceived as a European one, the company was then 'prepared to consider possible co-operation from outside Europe'. Many glittering inducements in 'the latest technology' have been offered to various nations in an endeavour to enlist them into the project. The production ACT, also known as Rafale-B, and navalized ACM are to have lighter and even more advanced airframes, with wing area reduced to 474ft² (44m²), cutting empty weight to only 18,739lb (8,500kg), though it is not immediately evident how this could be done. The engines are expected to be changed for new French augmented turbofans derived from the SNECMA M88, which, it is anticipated, will be smaller and lighter than the present American engine yet have a maximum thrust of 75kN (16,858lb/7,647kg). Dassault hope to obtain permission to build six prototypes of the definitive aircraft, four ACT and two ACM, though none is likely to fly before 1990. The ACM is expected to have non-folding wings, and to be launched using a ski-ramp. The company sees itself as being in head-on competition with EuroFighter GmbH in an attempt to win markets throughout the world estimated to encompass 'at least 1,000 aircraft' excluding the original developing country. India has signified a wish to share in development, despite that country's own project for an LCA (Light Combat Aircraft).

Dassault-Breguet Super Etendard

Origin: Avions Marcel Dassault-Breguet Aviation, France.
Type: Single-seat naval strike fighter.
Engine: One 11,265lb (5,110kg) thrust SNECMA Atar 8K-50 turbojet.
Dimensions: Span 31ft 5¾ in (9.6m); length 46ft 11½ in (14.31m); height 12ft 8in (3.85m); wing area 305.7ft² (28.4m²).
Weights: Empty 14,200lb (6,450kg); loaded 25,350lb (11,500kg).
Performance: Max speed (clean) 745mph (1,200km/h) at sea level, Mach 1 at altitude; initial climb rate 24,600ft (7,500m)/min; service ceiling 45,000ft (13,700m); radius (hi-lo-hi, one AM.39, one tank) 403 miles (650km).
Armament: Two 30mm DEFA cannon, each with 125 rounds; five pylons for weapon load with full internal fuel of 4,630lb (2,100kg); one AM.39 Exocet can be carried (right wing) with one tank (left).
History: First flight (converted Etendard) 28 October 1974; first delivery late 1977.
Users: Argentina, France, Iraq.

The French Aéronavale still uses the original Etendard IVM attack aircraft and IVP photo-reconnaissance machine, in each case often as a 'buddy' air refuelling tanker carrying a hose-reel pod. The replacement for the former is the Super Etendard. This is a very much updated aircraft, though with the advantage of some commonality with the earlier machine. Though called a strike fighter, the Super Etendard is used almost wholly in an air-to-surface role.

Equipment includes an Agave multimode radar which is fully adequate for most attacks on surface ships, a Sagem (Kearfott licence) inertial nav/attack system, a BF radar warning system and a DB-3141 ECM jammer pod. Free-fall bombs of 250 and 400kg sizes can be carried, but the chief anti-ship weapon is the AM.39 Exocet.

L'Aéronavale planned to buy 100 Super Etendards but inflation reduced the total to 71 in 1978–82. These equip Flotilles 11F and 14F at Landivisiau, 17F at Hyères and 12F at Landivisiau, the latter in the intercept role replacing the

Below: Two of the five Super Etendards delivered to the Argentine Navy prior to the invasion of the Falklands in April 1982.

Above: The first Super Etendard on test in 1978. Several ex-Aéronavale aircraft have been leased to Iraq in order to attack tankers in the Persian Gulf and related Iranian shore targets, and these have caused much havoc with bombs and Exocet missiles.

Crusader. The IVP remains in use but a reconnaissance version of the Super has long been projected. Super Etendard flotilles go to sea aboard the small and aged *Clemenceau* and *Foch,* to replace which two 33,000-tonne nuclear carriers are planned for the end of the century, the keel for the first, *Charles de Gaulle*, having been laid in 1986. By this time, the basic obsolescence of the Super Etendard had begun to show, and it is hoped to replace it by a navalised Rafale.

In 1982 Iraq tried to purchase Super Etendards armed with AM.39 missiles to bolster its capability against oil tankers in the war against Iran. There has been international pressure on France not to sell, and reopening the production line would be uneconomic, the last of 14 aircraft for Argentina having been delivered in early 1983. Nevertheless some 30 Iraqi personnel completed training on both the aircraft and missile in August 1983, at Landivisiau, and l'Aéronavale loaned five missile-armed Super Etendards from reserve stocks.

Below: Tailplane at full negative incidence, a Super Etendard taxies towards the catapult. Note the older Etendard IVM (right).

Dassault-Breguet/Dornier Alpha Jet, Lancier

Origin: Jointly Dassault-Breguet, France, and Dornier GmbH, West Germany, with assembly in France (previously at each company); co-production by Egyptian Government Factory 36, Helwan.

Type: Two-seat trainer and light strike/reconnaissance aircraft.

Engines: Two 2,976lb (1,350kg) thrust SNECMA/Turboméca Larzac C5 turbofans; (Lancier) 3,175lb (1,440kg) Larzac C20.

Dimensions: Span 20ft 10¾in (9.11m); length (exc any probe) 40ft 3¾in (12.29m); height 13ft 9in (4.2m); wing area 188.4ft² (17.5m²).

Weights: Empty (trainer) 7,374lb (3,345kg); loaded (clean) 11,023lb (5,000kg); (max) 16,535lb (7,500kg).

Performance: Max speed (clean) 576mph (927km/h) at sea level, 560mph (900km/h, Mach 0.85) at altitude; climb to 39,370ft (12,000m) less than 10min; service ceiling 48,000ft (14,630m); typical mission endurance 2hr 30min; ferry range (two external tanks) 1,827 miles (2,940km).

Armament: Optional for weapon training or combat missions, detachable belly fairing housing one 30mm DEFA or 27mm Mauser cannon, with 125 rounds; same centreline hardpoint and either one or two under each wing can be provided with pylons for max external load of 5,511lb (2,500kg), made up of tanks, weapons, recon pod, ECM or other devices.

History: First flight 26 October 1973; first production delivery late 1978.

Users: (Alpha Jet E) Belgium, Egypt, France, Ivory Coast, Morocco, Nigeria, Qatar, Togo; (A) West Germany; (alternative close-support version) Cameroun, Egypt.

In 1969 France and West Germany announced a collaborative programme for a jet trainer. After an industry competition the Alpha Jet was selected in 1970. The design was arranged with a high wing to give plenty of clearance for underwing stores, though this resulted in a narrow main landing gear track with the units folding into the fuselage. The basic Alpha Jet E, for training and light attack, has tandem staggered Martin-Baker seats, those for l'Armée de

Below: Regular Alpha Jet E trainers serving with l'Armée de l'Air's Escadre de Transformation 8 at Cazaux. These aircraft replaced Mystère IVAs in the weapon training role. All 175 Alpha Jets purchased for l'Armée de l'Air had been delivered by 1986.

l'Air being Mk 4s usable at zero height but not below 104mph (167km/h) airspeed, although Egypt, Belgium and Qatar have Mk 10 seats with zero/zero capability.

This model serves with l'Armée de l'Air (200 total) to equip Groupement-Ecole 314 Christian Martel at Tours, the *Patrouille de France* aerobatic team at Salon, the Centre d'Entrainement au Vol sans Visibilité and the 8e Escadre de Transformation at Cazaux. It is also used (33 supplied) by Belgium's Nos 7, 9 and 11 Sqns at St Truiden (St Trond).

The Federal German Luftwaffe uses a version in the close-support and reconnaissance roles. The Alpha Jet A has the Mauser gun, a pointed nose with pitot probe (aircraft length 43ft 5in/13.23m) and MBB-built Stencel seats. A total of 153 were supplied to three fighter-bomber wings, JaboG 49 at Fürstenfeldbruck, JaboG 43 at Oldenburg and JaboG 41 at Husum, each with 51 aircraft on strength. They are austerely equipped for attack missions in the European environment, though navigation systems are good and a HUD is provided. The LaCroix BOZ-10 chaff pod has been developed jointly by France and Germany and is expected to appear with these JaboGs. In the reconnaissance role a Super Cyclope pod can be carried with optical cameras, IR linescan and a decoy launcher. The Luftwaffe has 18 Alpha Jets in the weapon-training role at Beja, Portugal, the German total being 175.

The alternative close-support version has inertial navigation, a HUD, a laser ranger and a radar altimeter, and is co-produced at Helwan, Egypt, as the MS2, the original trainer being known as the MS1. Dassault-Breguet has itself developed this model further into the Lancier, with the more powerful Larzac C20 engine and enhanced pylon capability for tanks or Magic AAMs. In 1984 Helwan was producing both the MS1 and MS2 at the rate of two every three months, with the rear fuselage and control surfaces manufactured locally. No Lancier orders have been announced.

Below: This Alpha Jet has since 1985 been serving as the test-bed for the Lancier, the ultimate armed version for multiple combat roles. Though this particular machine does not have the planned Agave radar, it is seen carrying an Exocet anti-ship missile, tank, and two Magic AAMs. Should an export customer order the Lancier he would be able to dictate the avionic/weapon fit.

ENAER A-36 Halcón; CASA C-101 Aviojet

Origin: ENAER, Chile, under licence from CASA, Spain.

Type: Two-seat light attack aircraft.

Engine: One Garrett TFE731-5 turbofan rated at (normal) 4,300lb (1,950kg), (military power reserve) 4,700lb (2,132kg).

Dimensions: Span 34ft 9¼in (10.6m); length 41ft (12.5m); height 13ft 11¼in (4.25m); wing area 215.3ft² (20m²).

Weights: Empty 7,666lb (3,340kg); loaded (clean) 10,692lb (4,850kg), (with attack load) 13,890lb (6,300kg).

Performance: Max speed (clean, at 15,000ft/4,572m, with MPR engine thrust) 518mph (834km/h); initial climb rate (MPR) 5,300ft (1,615m)/min; service ceiling 42,000ft (12,800m); combat radius (lo-lo-lo, four 250kg bombs and 30mm gun, 3min over target) 322 miles (519km).

Armament: Internal fuselage bay houses numerous quick-change packs, including 30mm DEFA cannon pod with ammunition, or twin 12.7mm MG pod, laser designator, ECM jammers or reconnaissance camera group; six wing pylons for various stores up to total weight of 4,960lb (2,250kg).

History: First flight (CASA C-101 Aviojet) 27 June 1977, (C-101CC attack version) 16 November 1983.

User: Chile.

CASA of Spain began development of the C-101 Aviojet in 1975, and from 1980 a total of 88 aircraft were delivered to the EdA (Spanish Air Force) as E.25 Mirlo (Blackbird) trainers. MBB and Northrop assisted with the design, and an unusual feature is the incorporation of an internal bay for several kinds of weapons or mission equipment. The C-101BB is an armed export version with engine thrust increased from 3,500lb (1,587kg) to 3,700lb (1,678kg), and the C-101DD is an enhanced trainer first flown in 1985 with numerous upgraded avionics. The DD has the same powerplant as the C-101CC light attack aircraft, and it is this which is built under licence in Chile as the A-36.

Above: A prototype of the original CASA C-101 demonstrating its weapons capability with twin 12.7mm machine gun pods and six 500lb GP bombs on the wing pylons.

Chile, also a major user of the C-101BB, initially ordered 20 A-36 Halcóns, the last 19 being assembled (and increasingly manufactured) by ENAER. The FAC (Chilean Air Force) also received the four Spanish-built prototypes. Previously, ENAER had licence-built 13 of 17 of the C-101BB version.

The Halcón (Hawk) replaces the Cessna A-37 Dragonfly as the standard light attack and reconnaissance aircraft in Chilean service. Deliveries began to the 1st Air Group in late 1983. The A-36, like the T-36 Halcón (C-101BB) trainer, is characterized by an unswept wing, staggered Martin-Baker 10L zero/zero seats, powered ailerons, a belly door-type airbrake, and very comprehensive avionics and equipment. The high bypass ratio turbofan engine confers excellent range and endurance, and the Halcón, like the original Spanish C-101 versions, has proven most satisfactory and popular in service.

Below: Similar to the Halcón, the C-101DD is an enhanced aircraft with doppler radar and Ferranti HUD and weapon-aiming computer. Here it has a 30mm DEFA gun, two bombs and four rocket launchers.

EuroFighter

Origin: EuroFighter Jagdflugzeug GmbH, an international company based in Munich.
Type: Multirole air-combat fighter.
Engines: Two Eurojet EJ.200 augmented turbofans each in 90 kilonewtons (20,230lb/9,177kg) thrust class. See text.
Dimensions: Not finalized; (EAP) span 38ft 7½ in (11.77m); length 57ft 6¼ in (17.53m); height 18ft 1¼ in (5.52m); wing area 520ft² (48.3m²). EuroFighter wing area is to be 538ft² (50m²).
Weights: Equipped empty 21,495lb (9,750kg); max loaded about 40,000lb (18,144kg).
Performance: Max speed (with weapons, at high altitude) over 1,320mph (2,135km/h, Mach 2 +); ceiling about 60,000ft (18,288m); initial climb rate over 50,000ft (15,240m)/min; combat radius greater than most current fighters.
Armament: Provision for a gun; in air-combat role, typically four AIM-120A Amraam missiles and two AIM-132 Asraam missiles. See text.
History: First flight of EAP demonstrator 8 August 1986; EuroFighter might fly in 1988—89; target in-service date 1995.
Users: West Germany, Italy, Spain, UK (RAF).

Below: A beautiful portrait of the British Aerospace EAP which is providing technical underpinning for the planned EFA. The mock-up missiles carried here are four BAe Dynamics Sky Flash, with two AIM-132A Asraam advanced short-range weapons outboard.

Following many years of study, it was generally decided in the early 1980s that the next-generation fighter for the major NATO nations of Western Europe should be a conventional machine requiring fixed air bases for its operation. Again by general agreement, the configuration was finalized as an unstable canard with a very large delta wing, the latest cockpit displays, all-digital avionics including a quad-redundant fly-by-wire flight control system, twin augmented turbofan engines and low-drag conformal weapon carriage. It was hoped that a multinational go-ahead could be agreed, but in the event in 1982 the British Ministry of Defence and British industry jointly funded a single demonstrator of many of the new technologies. This single aircraft, the EAP (Experimental Aircraft Programme), incorporates parts contributed by hundreds of companies, many of them being in Italy (which produced the complete left wing) and West Germany (which provided mainly avionics).

EAP is not to be regarded as a prototype of the eventual EuroFighter but as a valuable research tool, the design of which is as close as possible to that agreed for the EuroFighter. Its engines are Turbo-Union RB.199 Mk 104D turbofans of about 18,000lb (8,165kg) thrust each, as fitted to the Tornado F.3 but with reversers removed. The structure is a mix of advanced light alloys, superplastic-formed titanium, glassfibre, carbon fibre (for almost the entire basic wings and foreplanes) and some other composites. Control surfaces comprise the foreplanes, inboard and outboard wing flaperons, leading-edge droops and the rudder. All wing surfaces are computer-scheduled, and all controls are computer-controlled hundreds of times per second to guide what has deliberately been made an unstable aircraft. EAP is certainly the most agile fighter ever built. A prominent design feature is the use of a large ventral engine inlet, with a hinged lower lip ('varicowl'). Engine airflow is improved at high angles of attack, in violent manoeuvres, by extending the giant wing for- ▶

▶ wards in a so-called apex section above the inlet, which is well below the fuselage. Speedbrakes are large door-type surfaces hinged above the rear fuselage on each side of the fin.

Everything possible has been done in the EAP to reproduce the qualities and features of the eventual EuroFighter. It carries four radar-guided medium-range missiles (Sky Flash or Amraam) under the fuselage and rear wing root, and two Asraam dogfight missiles on pylons well inboard from the wing tips. The EuroFighter will probably have several stores attachments under each wing, and electronic-warfare pods on the wing tips. Its radar will fit into a slightly slimmer nose, and the vertical tail will probably be smaller and simpler.

EuroFighter GmbH has been formed jointly by British Aerospace (right wing, front fuselage and canard, 33 per cent), MBB of West Germany (centre fuselage and fin, 33, with Dornier as co-partner), Aeritalia (left wing and rear fuselage, 21) and CASA of Spain (share of right wing and rear fuselage, 13). The new engines will be produced by the Eurojet consortium owned by Rolls-Royce, MTU, Fiat and Sener of Spain. They will be based on a new Rolls-Royce engine, the XG-40, now on test. This is slightly more powerful than the RB.199, and considerably simpler. Full engineering development of the EuroFighter was to begin in early 1987. Eight prototypes will be built, meeting the requirements of the four nations whose air forces will initially require about 800 aircraft. These will be assembled in all four countries, at Warton, Manching, Turin and Madrid, though there will be no duplication of parts-manufacture. Avionics and weapons will to some degree be national fits. Thus, both in management structure and in the exact tailoring of the final aircraft, the EuroFighter programme will follow guidelines set by Panavia with the Tornado.

Above: From this angle it is just possible to see that the EAP's fantastic wing is devoid of any straight lines, most of the curved leading edge being occupied by powered droop flaps.

Below: The agreed EuroFighter configuration has a smaller and more refined vertical tail, a slimmer nose, and streamlined ECM pods on the wing tips. AIM-120A Amraams nestle against the fuselage.

Fairchild Republic A-10 Thunderbolt II

Origin: Fairchild Republic Co, USA.
Type: Close-support attack aircraft.
Engines: Two 9,065lb (4,112kg) thrust General Electric TF34-100 turbofans.
Dimensions: Span 57ft 6in (17.53m); length 53ft 4in (16.26m); height 14ft 8in (4.47m); wing area 506ft² (47m²).
Weights: Empty 21,519lb (9,761kg); forward airstrip weight (no fuel but four Mk 82 bombs and 750 rounds) 32,730lb (14,846kg); max 50,000lb (22,680kg).
Performance: Max speed (max weight) 423mph (681km/h); cruising speed (sea level) 345mph (555km/h); stabilized speed below 8,000ft (2,440m) in 45° dive at 35,125lb (15,932kg) weight, 299mph (481km/h); max climb at 31,790lb (14,420kg) basic design weight, 6,000ft (1,828m)/min; service ceiling not stated; take-off run to 50ft (15m) at max weight 4,000ft (1,220m); operating radius in CAS mission with 1.8hr loiter and reserves 288 miles (463km); radius for single deep-strike penetration 620 miles (1,000km); ferry range with allowances 2,542 miles (4,091km).
Armament: One GAU-8/A Avenger 30mm seven-barrel gun with 1,174 rounds; total external ordnance load 16,000lb (7,257kg) hung on 11 pylons, three side-by-side on body and four under each wing; several hundred combinations of stores up to individual weight of 5,000lb (2,268kg), with max total weight 14,638lb (6,640kg) with full internal fuel.
History: First flight (YA-10A) 10 May 1972, (production A-10A) 21 October 1975.
User: USA (AF, ANG).

Until 1967 the USAF had never bothered to procure a close-support aircraft, instead flying CAS missions with fighters and attack machines. With the A-10, the emphasis was placed on the ability to operate from short, unpaved, front-line airstrips, to carry an exceptional load of weapons — in particular a very powerful high-velocity gun — and to withstand prolonged exposure to

gunfire from the ground. Avionics were left to a minimum, but a few extra items are now being added.

The A-10A is larger than most tactical attack aircraft and carefully designed as a compromise between capability and low cost. As an example of the latter many of the major parts, including flaps, main landing gears and movable tail surfaces, are interchangeable left/right, and systems and engineering features were designed with duplication and redundancy to survive parts being shot away. The unusual engine location minimizes the infrared signature and makes the aircraft simple to fly with one engine inoperative.

Weapon pylons were added from tip to tip, but the chief tank-killing ordnance is the gun, the most powerful (in terms of muzzle horsepower) ever mounted in an aircraft, firing milk-bottle size rounds at rates hydraulically controlled at 2,100 or 4,200 per minute. The basic aircraft has a HUD, a good communications fit and both tacan and inertial navigation. RHAWS and ECM have been internal from the start, but jammer pods are hung externally.

In 1979 Fairchild flew a company-funded NAW (night/adverse weather) demonstrator. Both the regular and NAW aircraft carry a Pave Penny laser seeker pod under the nose, vital for laser-guided munitions, and the NAW also had a Ferranti laser ranger, a Texas Instruments FLIR (forward-looking infrared), a GE low-light TV and many other items including a Westinghouse multimode radar with WSO display. It is probable that during the rest of the decade A-10As will be brought at least close to the NAW standard, with the LANTIRN pod, though the two-seat NAW itself was never funded. A-10A funding was terminated in 1982 at a total of 707 aircraft for inventory.

In service with the 57th TTW, four regular TFWs (the 23rd, 81st, 354th and 355th) and the 66th FWS of the USAF, and with the 174th TFW and four TFGs (103rd, 104th, 128th and 175th) of the ANG, the A-10A has proved generally popular and effective. The only worry is the attrition rate, caused by aircraft hitting the ground during operations at low levels.

Below: A brace of A-10As — often called Warthogs rather than by the official name — from the 354th TFW at Myrtle Beach. Previously a Corsair II outfit, the 354th are used to going anywhere at short notice. The A-10's massive 30mm GAU-8/A gun — the muzzle protrudes beneath the nose — is the most potent ever in a production aircraft.

FMA IA 58/66 Pucará

Origin: Fabrica Militar de Aviones, Argentina.
Type: Close-support attack and reconnaissance aircraft.
Engines: Two turboprops, (58) 988shp Turboméca Astazou XVIG, (66) 1,000shp Garrett TPE331-11-601W.
Dimensions: Span 47ft 6¾in (14.5m), length 46ft 9¼in (14.253m), height overall 17ft 7in (5.362m); wing area 326.1ft² (30.3m²).
Weights: Empty (58A) 8,900lb (4,037kg), (66) 8,862lb (4,020kg); max 14,991lb (6,800kg).
Performance: (Both) Max speed (9,840ft/3,000m) 310mph (500km/h); economical cruise 267mph (430km/h); take-off to 50ft (15m) at 12,125lb (5,500kg) 2,313ft (705m); landing from 50ft (15m) 1,978ft (603m); attack radius (max external weapons, 10 per cent reserve fuel, hi-lo-hi) 155 miles (250km), (1,764lb/800kg weapons, external fuel) 559 miles (900km); ferry range 1,890 miles (3,042km).
Armament: Two 20mm Hispano HS804 each with 270 rounds and four 7.62mm FN Browning each with 900 rounds all firing ahead; up to 3,307lb (1,500kg) of wide range of stores carried on three pylons, with individual stores up to 2,205lb (1,000kg), examples including 12 bombs of 276lb (125kg), 12 large napalm tanks, three 1,102lb (500kg) DA bombs, seven 19 x 2.75in (70mm) rocket pods or a cannon pod and two 72.5gal (330l) drop tanks.
History: First flight (prototype) 20 August 1969, (58A) 8 November 1974, (66) late 1980.
Users: Argentina, Central African Republic, Uruguay, Venezuela.

The Pucará, named after an early hilltop type of stone fortress, was influenced by the US interest in light turboprop COIN aircraft in the early 1960s. Intended for use against unsophisticated forces, and in fact ordered by the FAA (Argentine Air Force) for suppressing internal disorders, it was planned to have considerable firepower yet operate from austere airstrips with the minimum of ground support.

Features include pilot and co-pilot in staggered Martin-Baker zero/zero seats, carefully disposed armour, and equipment for operation by night but not in adverse weather. There is good avionics provision for communications

Right: A standard IA 58A at a simulated 'advanced front-line base' devoid of proper facilities. Despite its poor showing in the Falklands War, the Pucará remains valid for quelling insurrections.

Below: Another standard IA 58A, being flown without a back-seater. As noted in the text, development is now aimed mainly at future single-seat versions, both new and rebuilds of existing machines.

and navigation, and ILS is standard, but weapon aiming is visual. Weather radar is an option.

In the South Atlantic War in spring 1982 Pucarás played a major role in the Falklands, being able to use various airstrips through the islands. Despite their good weapon load and inflight agility, the 20 island-based machines accomplished little beyond shooting down a British Army Scout AH.1 helicopter on 28 May. None survived; six were brought to Britain and one was carefully evaluated at Boscombe Down.

Meanwhile, production of 108 for the FAA was believed completed in 1986, the 90th being accepted in June 1983. Continuing production is for export, and a Libyan mission evaluated the IA 66 export model in spring 1983. Most of the missions flown over the Falklands were by single pilots, and a single-seat IA 66 is seen as the most likely definitive model. FMA flew an IA 58B with 30mm guns and upgraded avionics, and planned a turbofan version, but dropped both.

Following experience in the Falklands many Pucarás have been converted into single-seaters. In 1985 FMA flew the first of a definitive improved version, the IA 58C. Also a single-seater, this has a 30mm DEFA 5-53 gun in the nose, with 270 rounds. Other changes include AAM (usually Matra Magic) launchers under the wing tips; provision for heavier and more varied weapon loads including two Argentinian Martin Pescador tactical attack missiles; a larger and better protected cockpit; considerably upgraded avionics, including Omega/VLF navigation, a low-level radio altimeter, better instruments, a radar warning system, a HUD and computing sight, and an IFF; and comprehensive ECM, including internal or pod-mounted flares, chaff or electronic jammers. The engines are still Astazou XVIGs, but with IR-suppressed jetpipes and a self-start capability.

General Dynamics F-16 Fighting Falcon

Origin: General Dynamics, Fort Worth, Texas.

Type: (A,C,N) Multirole fighter, (B, D) operational fighter/trainer, (G) reconnaissance aircraft.

Engine: (A,B) One 23,840lb (10,814kg) thrust Pratt & Whitney F100-200 augmented turbofan, (C,D) alternatively 23,450lb (10,637kg) thrust F100-220, or 27,600lb (12,519kg) thrust General Electric F110-100 augmented turbofan; (N) F110 only.

Dimensions: (Same for all production versions) Span (over empty missile launchers) 31ft (9.45m); length 49ft 3in (15.01m); height 16ft 8½in (5.09m); wing area 300ft² (27.87m²).

Weights: Empty (A) 16,234lb (7,364kg), (C) 16,794lb (7,618kg), (D) 17,408lb (7,896kg); max loaded (A,B) 35,400lb (16,057kg), (C,D) 37,500lb (17,010kg).

Performance: Max speed (all, AAMs only) 1,350mph (2,173km/h, Mach 2.05) at 40,000ft (12,190m), (sea level) 910mph (1,470km/h, Mach 1.2); initial climb rate (AAMs only) 50,000ft (15,240m)/min; service ceiling, over 50,000ft (15,240m); tactical radius (A, six Mk 82, internal fuel, hi-lo-hi) 340 miles (547km); ferry range 2,415 miles (3,890km).

Armament: One M61A-1 20mm gun with 500/515 rounds; centreline pylon for 250gal (1,136l) drop tank or 2,200lb (998kg) bomb, inboard wing pylons for 4,500lb (2,041kg) each, middle wing pylons for 3,500lb (1,587kg) each, outer wing pylons for 700lb (318kg) each (being uprated under MSIP-1 to 3,500lb), wing-tip pylons for 425lb (193kg), all ratings being at 9g; normal max load 11,950lb (5,420kg) for 9g.

History: First flight (YF-16) 20 January 1974, (production F-16A) 7 August 1978; service delivery (A) 17 August 1978.

Users: Belgium, Denmark, Egypt, Greece, Israel, South Korea, Netherlands, Norway, Pakistan, Singapore, Thailand, Turkey, USA (AF, ANG), Venezuela. (In 1984 a request from the Chinese People's Republic for two squadrons of F-16s was being considered, and four other sales were in view.)

Below: No fewer than 2,795 F-16s are expected to be delivered to the US Air Force and Reserve Forces at rates reaching 216 per year.

Above: In a sustained vertical climb (possible whenever weight is less than available thrust) the only real problem is the pilot's wish to lean forward so as not to lie head-down in the seat!

Starting as a small technology demonstrator, the F-16 swiftly matured into a brilliantly capable multirole fighter which in the eyes of most observers is number one in the Western world. Basic features include a fixed wing tapered on the leading edge, with automatic variable camber from hinged leading and trailing edges, a slab horizontal tail, a single large engine of the type already used in the F-15, fed by a plain ventral inlet without any variable geometry, a modern cockpit with a reclining seat, a sidestick force-transducer controller linked to FBW flight controls and an overall concept of relaxed static stability which even today represents an exceptional application of the CCV concept. ▶

▶ At the time of its design the F-16's ability to sustain 9g in prolonged turns was unique, and turns at 5.5g can be made with a theoretical external stores load of 20,450lb (9,276kg), roughly the same as the original clean gross weight! In service the usual maximum weapon load is as given in the specification.

It was in January 1975 that the F-16 was selected as a major type for the USAF inventory, with the total procurement set at 2,795 of the A, B, C and D versions, the B and D being two-seaters, with full avionics and weapons but with 17 per cent less fuel.

In June 1975 the F-16 was selected for Belgium, Denmark, the Netherlands and Norway, mainly to replace the F-104. These European countries insisted on substantial industrial offsets, and a multinational manufacturing programme was set up to build production aircraft.

By far the largest user is the USAF. This chose the 388th TFW at Hill AFB, Utah, as lead operator, and Hill has also served as a principal logistics centre and training base for the international F-16 programme. Other F-16 units in the USAF include the 56th and 58th TTWs, the 8th, 50th 363rd, 401st and 474th TFWs, the *Thunderbirds* display team, the 169th TFG of the ANG and the 466th TFS of the AFRes.

The FAB (Belgian Air Force) has 116 aircraft, with a follow-on order for 44, with two squadrons each at Beauvechain and Kleine Brogel. Egypt has 40, equipping 232 Fighter Brigade at Inchas, with plans for two similar brigades to be based at Al Mansurah and Abu Hammad. Israel has 150 F-16s, eight of which, each armed with two 2,000lb (907kg) bombs, flew a very long dogleg mission at low level in June 1981 to destroy the Iraqi nuclear reactor at Osirak with pinpoint accuracy. Israeli F-16s have also seen a lot of action over the Lebanon, principally against Syrian Air Force MiG-23 'Floggers'.

Above: Nearly all export customers have announced one or more repeat orders, Egypt being typical with 40 followed by a further 40. Though the F-4E remains important, and some Soviet types have been restored to active service, the F-16 is today by far the most significant combat aircraft in the Egyptian Air Force.

Above right: Pulling about 5g in a public demonstration of F-16 agility. The sharp-lipped wing root extensions create violent writhing vortices which spiral back across the wing, re-energizing the boundary layer and keeping the wing unstalled and effective at high AOA.

Right: Shown in clean condition, the two-seaters — this was the first Belgian F-16B — are classed as fighter/trainers, with full combat capability. The USAF plans to replace the RF-4C Phantom with an advanced two-seater designated F-16G, with new sensors and navaids.

South Korea received 36 aircraft from 1986. The Netherlands has an initial batch of 102, equipping two squadrons at Leeuwarden, two at Volkel, and a third (No 306) at Volkel tasked in the recon role carrying a multisensor pod on the centreline. Further batches have since been ordered of 22, 18, 12 and 57, the final delivery being in early 1992. Norway bought 72 F-16s, and Denmark 58 followed by a further 12. Pakistan received 40, completed in January 1986, and has been negotiating for a further 60; orders by Singapore, Thailand, Greece and Turkey are listed later.

In 1980 the US Air Force launched the MSIP (multistaged improvement programme), to extend the multirole all-weather capabilty of the basic aircraft. Since late 1981 all aircraft have wiring and avionics system architecture for later updating with LANTIRN night and attack pods, one on each side of the inlet duct, the ASPJ (airborne self-protection jammer) EW system, the APG-68 radar, a giant GEC Avionics wide-angle head-up cockpit display, and the AIM-120A Amraam. The latter rectifies the curious lack of a radar-guided AAM which cost the F-16 several export sales to the F-18 Hornet. The upgraded aircraft, now operational with the USAF, is the F-16C, the F-16D being the two-seat version.

General Dynamics have evaluated an F-16 with the F101DFE engine, as a result of which the F110 engine is now in production to power future F-16s, the initial 1984 buy being 120 units. The resulting more powerful (and in other ways superior) aircraft are still designated F-16C and D, the F100 and F110 being alternative installations. All Israeli F-16C/D aircraft have the F110 engine, as do 160 for Turkey, 40 for Greece and 26 F-16N adversary aircraft for the US Navy. The F-16G is a two-seat multisensor reconnaissance version for the USAF, planned to replace the RF-4C Phantom in the recon role.

General Dynamics F-16 developments

Origin: General Dynamics, Fort Worth, Texas.
Type: (F-16F) Dual-role air-defence/ground-attack fighter.
Engine: (F) 27,600lb (12,519kg) thrust General Electric F110-100 augmented turbofan, (AFTI) 23,840lb (10,814kg) thrust Pratt & Whitney F100-200 augmented turbofan.
Dimensions: (F) Span 34ft 2¼in (10.43m); length 54ft 2in (16.51m); height 17ft 7in (5.36m); wing area 663ft² (61.59m²).
Weights: (F) Design mission weight 43,000lb (19,504kg); max loaded 48,000lb (21,772kg).
Performance: (F) Max level speed (hi-altitude), Mach 2; max mission range, over 2,879 miles (4,630km).
Armament: (F) External stores load of 15,000lb (6,804kg), carried with very low drag in conformal launchers.
History: First flight (F) 3 July 1982, (AFTI) 10 July 1982; planned first flight of F-16F, 1989.
Users: Not yet funded for inventory.

The AFTI (Advanced Fighter Technology Integration) F-16 is a basically standard F-16A pre-production aircraft which in 1979–82 was subjected to a complete rebuild to fly a very challenging research and demonstration programme. The chief external modification was the addition of two downward-sloping canard foreplanes on the inlet duct, which are used as primary control surfaces linked with the other movable surfaces into a very advanced computer-controlled FBW (fly-by-wire) system. Of CCV (control-configured vehicle) type, the AFTI is a basically highly agile, unstable aircraft which, unlike previous fighters, can fly in a straight line whilst pointing to the left or right, or up or down, or alternatively travel vertically up or down, or sideways to left or right, without changing its attitude or banking the wings. Its three computers handle some 500,000 operations per second. This aircraft is assisting the US industry to design a future ATF (Advanced Tactical Fighter) for the USAF.

Above: Not intended as a production aircraft, the AFTI/F-16 is perhaps the world's most complicated technology test-bed. In conjunction with simulators on the ground, it is being used to perfect new ways of flying and manoeuvring. In future the limiting factor will almost always be what the pilot can reasonably take.

The F-16F is a planned future production version of the two F-16XL research aircraft, one powered by the F100 and the second a two-seater powered by the F110 engine, which flew in 1982. Distinguished by a giant wing of tailless 'cranked arrow' shape, the XLs demonstrated amazing superiority over the regular F-16. Though the fuselage was lengthened by only 4ft 8in (1.42m), the internal fuel capacity was increased by no less than 85 per cent, and there was also room for more avionics.

Below: So far General Dynamics has built just two XLs, this example being the single-seater with the P&W engine. Enhancement of performance and weapon load is colossal, and development is continuing. The GE-engined two-seater has tested disruptive and confusing paint schemes, which can have a significant effect in close combat.

General Dynamics F-111

Origin: General Dynamics, Fort Worth, Texas.
Type: (A,C,D,E,F) All-weather attack aircraft; (FB) strategic attack aircraft.
Engines: Two Pratt & Whitney TF30 afterburning turbofans as follows: (A, C) 18,500lb (8,390kg) TF30-3, (D, E) 19,600lb (8,891kg) TF30-9, (FB) 20,350lb (9,231kg) TF30-7, (F) 25,100lb (11,385kg) TF30-100.
Dimensions: Span (fully spread) (A,D,E,F) 63ft (19.2m), (C,FB) 70ft (21.34m), (fully swept) (A,D,E,F) 31ft 11½in (9.74m), (C,FB) 33ft 11in (10.34m); length 73ft 6in (22.4m); wing area (A,D,E,F, gross, 16°) 525ft² (48.77m²).
Weights: Empty (A) 46,172lb (20,943kg), (C) 47,300lb (21,455kg), (D) 49,090lb (22,267kg), (E) about 47,000lb (21,319kg), (F) 47,481lb (21,537kg), (FB) close to 50,000lb (22,680kg); loaded (A) 91,500lb (41,500kg), (D,E) 92,500lb (41,954kg), (C,F) 100,000lb (45,360kg), (FB) 114,300lb (51,846kg).
Performance: Max speed (36,000ft/11,000m, clean, max afterburner) (A,C,D,E) 1,450mph (2,335km/h, Mach 2.2), (FB) 1,320mph (2,135km/h, Mach 2), (F) 1,650mph (2,655km/h, Mach 2.5); cruising speed (penetration) 571mph (919km/h); service ceiling (combat weight, max afterburner) (A) 51,000ft (15,500m), (F) 60,000ft (18,290m); range (max

internal fuel) (A, D) 3,165 miles (5,093km), (F) 2,925 miles (4,707km); take-off run (A) 4,000ft (1,219m), (F) under 3,000ft (914m), (FB) 4,700ft (1,433m).

Armament: Internal weapons bay for two B43 bombs or (D,F) one B43 and one M61 gun; three pylons under each wing (four inboard swivelling with wing, outers being fixed and usable only at 16°, otherwise being jettisoned) for max external load of 31,500lb (14,288kg); (FB only) provision for up to six SRAM, two internal.

History: First flight 21 December 1964; service delivery (A) June 1967.

User: (C) Australia, (others) USA (AF).

Basic features of the F-111 include a variable-sweep 'swing wing' (the first in production in the world) with limits of 16° and 72.5°, with exceptional high-lift devices, side-by-side seating for the pilot and right-seat navigator (usually also a pilot, though dual control is not fitted), large main gears with low-pressure tyres for no-flare landings on soft strips (these prevent the carriage of ordnance on fuselage pylons), a small internal weapons bay, very great internal ▶

Below: Two F-111D attack aircraft of the 27th TFW, from Cannon AFB. This version has complex Mk II avionics, resulting in a cockpit grossly different from those of the A, E and F models.

▶ fuel capacity (typically 5,022 US gal/19,010l), and emergency escape by jettisoning the entire crew compartment, which has its own parachutes and can serve as a survival shelter or boat.

General Dynamics built 141 of the F-111A version, and it is planned to update this version by fitting a digital computer to the original analog-type AJQ-20A nav/bomb system, together with the Air Force standard INS and a new control/display system. The F-111E was similar but had minor improvements, including engines of slightly greater power; 94 were delivered and survivors equip the 20th TFW at Upper Heyford, England. These are to receive the same updates as the A.

Next came the F-111D, with larger engine inlets and a different avionics system of a basically digital nature, including the APQ-30 attack radar, APN-189 doppler and HUDs for both crew members. The 96 built have always equipped the 27th TFW at Cannon AFB, New Mexico. The F-111F has improved avionics and engines, and equips the 48th TFW at Lakenheath, England. Some of these aircraft have the Pave Tack pod, normally stowed in the weapons bay but rotated out on a cradle for use. This provides a day/night all-weather capability to acquire, track, designate and hit surface targets using EO, IR or laser guided weapons.

The long-span FB-111A was bought to replace the B-58 and early models of B-52 in SAC, though the rising price resulted in a cut in procurement from 210 to 76, which entered service in October 1969. It has so-called Mk IIB avionics, derived from those of the D but configured for SAC missions using nuclear bombs or SRAMs. The FB equips SAC's 380th BW at Plattsburgh AFB, NY, and the 509th at Pease, New Hampshire.

The RAAF purchased 24 F-111Cs, which have the long-span wing and strengthened landing gear of the FB, but are otherwise F-111As with the original engine and inlet duct. The RAAF decided to have its own reconnaissance pallet developed by GD, and four F-111Cs have been fitted with cameras, IR linescan, TV, optical sights and sensor controls and displays in the right-hand cockpit. Four F-111Cs lost have been replaced by F-111As bought second-hand. The RAAF has evaluated various sensors and missiles for use in the maritime and anti-ship role.

In October 1986 GD began updating the avionics of all 381 aircraft in the USAF inventory, under a basic six-year, $1.1 billion contract. GE will provide new attack radars, TI new TFRs (terrain-following radars) and other suppliers new (but mainly off-the-shelf) navigation, communications, IFF and EW subsystems.

Above: Three F-111C bombers of the RAAF sweeping round in a turn in the Brisbane area. They have the same long-span wings as the Strategic Air Command FB-111A, but avionics resemble the F-111A's.

Left: The slight ventral bulge betrays this Australian machine as one of the four aircraft converted as RF-111Cs for reconnaissance.

Below: Easily the best attack version, the F-111F, used by Lakenheath's 48th TFW, can carry Pave Tack and GBU-15 smart bombs.

Grumman A-6 Intruder, EA-6B Prowler

Origin: Grumman Corporation, USA.

Type: (A-6A, B, C, E, F) Two-seat carrier-based all-weather attack aircraft; (EA-6A) two-seat ECM/attack aircraft; (EA-6B) four-seat ECM aircraft; (KA-6D) two-seat air-refuelling tanker.

Engines: (A-6E) Two 9,300lb (4,218kg) thrust Pratt & Whitney J52-8A turbojets; (EA-6B) two 11,200lb (5,080kg) J52-408; (A-6F) two 10,700lb (4,854kg) General Electric F404-400D turbofans.

Dimensions: Span 53ft (16.15m); length (except EA-6B) 54ft 7in (16.64m), (EA-6B) 59ft 5in (18.11m); height (A-6A, A-6C, KA-6D) 15ft 7in (4.75m), (A-6E, A-6F, EA-6A and B) 16ft 3in (4.95m); wing area 528.9ft² (49.1m²).

Weights: Empty (A-6A), 25,684lb (11,650kg), (EA-6A) 27,769lb (12,596kg), (EA-6B) 34,581lb (15,686kg), (A-6E) 25,630lb (11,625kg); max loaded (A-6A and E) 60,400lb (27,397kg), (EA-6B) 58,500lb (26,535kg).

Performance: Max speed (A-6A, clean) 685mph (1,102km/h) at sea level or 625mph (1,006km/h, Mach 0.94) at height, (EA-6A) over 630mph (1,014km/h), (EA-6B) 599mph (964km/h) at sea level, (A-6E) 648mph (1,043km/h) at sea level; initial climb rate (A-6E, clean) 8,600ft (2,621m)/min; service ceiling (A-6A) 41,660ft (12,700m), (A-6E) 44,600ft (13,595m), (EA-6B) 39,000ft (11,582m); range with full combat load (A-6E) 1,077 miles (1,733km).

Armament: (All attack versions, including EA-6A) Five stores locations each rated at 3,600lb (1,633kg) with max total load of 15,000lb (6,804kg); typical load thirty 500lb (227kg) bombs or up to four Harpoon anti-ship missiles; (EA-6B) none.

History: First flight (YA2F-1) 19 April 1960; service acceptance (A-6A) 1 February 1963; first flight (EA-6A) 1963, (KA-6D) 23 May 1966, (EA-6B) 25 May 1968, (A-6E) 27 February 1970, (A-6F) 1987.

User: USA (Navy, Marine Corps).

Below: This A-6E, from Carrier Air Wing CVW-3, has the TRAM turret under its nose. Note the swirling steam from the catapult, and also the EA-6B Prowler parked at extreme left.

Above: A quartet of A-6Es, all with the TRAM turret, from the carrier _Dwight D Eisenhower_. All have a centreline tank, the nearest has Sidewinders, and the next aircraft along (160997) appears overleaf. Over 200 A-6Es have been upgraded to TRAM standards.

Despite its seemingly outdated concept, the A-6 Intruder will remain in low-rate production throughout the foreseeable future as the standard equipment of all the heavy attack squadrons of the US Navy and Marine Corps.

The basic characteristics of all aircraft of the family include a conventional long-span wing with almost full-span flaps on both the leading and trailing edges. Ahead of the trailing-edge flaps are 'flaperons', used as lift spoilers and ailerons, while the tips contain split airbrakes which are fully opened on each carrier landing. Plain turbojets were used, and these remained in all successive versions up to the A-6F. The nose is occupied by a giant radar array, with a fixed FR probe above on the centreline in front of the side-by-side cockpit with Martin-Baker seats (slightly inclined and staggered) which can be tilted back to reduce fatigue. ▶

Above: A-6E No 160997 is seen here again minus TRAM turret but in low-contrast paint, and carrying the remarkable assortment of tank, rocket lauchers, Shrike anti-radar missile and Snakeye bombs!

▶ Like all Grumman products the A-6 soon gained a reputation for unbreakable strength. The internal fuel load of 15,939lb (7,230kg), with the option of 8,020lb (3,638kg) in four drop tanks, proved adequate to counteract the basically poor fuel economy of the engines.

Grumman delivered 482 of the original A-6A model, ending in December 1969, and 62 of these were converted into KA-6D air-refuelling tankers which can transfer over 21,000lb (9,526kg) of fuel through their hose reels. The KA-6D remains the standard tanker of the fourteen Carrier Air Wings, with a limited attack capability and equipment for use as an air/sea rescue control platform. The A-6A, B and C are no longer in use, the standard attack model being the A-6E. This has new radar, the Norden APQ-148 replacing two radars in earlier versions, as well as an IBM/Fairchild computer-backed attack and weapon-delivery system.

In 1974 an A-6E was fitted with the TRAM (Target Recognition and Attack Multisensor) package, comprising a stabilized chin turret containing a FLIR and a laser interlinked with the radar for detection, identification and weapon-guidance at greater ranges in adverse conditions. Other updates with TRAM include the Litton ASN-92 CAINS (Carrier Aircraft Inertial Navigation System), a new CNI suite and automatic carrier landing. A total of 228 Intruders are being modified to A-6E TRAM standard.

It was planned to deploy 318 A-6Es, but production has been continued with new airframes being produced at six a year until 1987. It is then planned to switch to the A-6F with new engines of lighter weight and much better fuel economy, and completely upgraded avionics including the same computers and multifunction cockpit displays as the F-14D Tomcat. The F has a new (Boeing) wing, also to be retrofitted to all other front-line Intruders. Production F deliveries are due from 1990.

The EA-6B Prowler is the standard electronic warfare platform of the Navy Carrier Air Wings and Marine Corps. Though it is based on the airframe of the

Right: The cockpit of the EA-6B Prowler accommodates the pilot (at left front) and three electronic warfare officers to beat the enemy. This model represents a considerable redesign of the basic Intruder.

A-6E, with local reinforcement to cater for the increased weights, fatigue life and 5.5g load factor, it is gutted of attack avionics and instead houses the AIL ALQ-99 tactical jamming system, which covers all anticipated hostile emitter frequency bands. Surveillance receivers are grouped in the fairing on the fin, and the active jammers are mounted in up to five external pods, each energized by a nose windmill generator and containing two (fore/aft) transmitters covering one of seven selected frequency bands.

To manage the equipment a crew of four is carried, comprising a pilot (left front), an ECM officer (right front) to manage navigation, communications, defensive ECM and chaff/flare dispensing, and two more ECMOs (rear seats) who can each detect, assign, adjust and monitor the jammers.

All VAQ (fixed-wing EW) squadrons of the Navy fly the EA-6B, as do the three Marine EW squadrons. Production at six aircraft per year is continuing to 1990. All in service have been updated with new avionics in two stages of ICAP (increased capability), and Norden is supplying about 10 advanced APS-130 navigation radars for retrofit to existing Prowlers. During the rest of the decade Grumman has to define a further update stage for the EA-6B, with most of the A-6F features.

Grumman F-14 Tomcat

Origin: Grumman Corporation, USA.
Type: Two-seat carrier-based multirole fighter.
Engines: (F-14A) Two 20,900lb (9,480kg) thrust Pratt & Whitney TF30-412A afterburning turbofans; (A, deliveries since 1983) two 20,900lb (9,480kg) thrust Pratt & Whitney TF30-414A afterburning turbofans; (A Plus, D) two 27,600lb (12,519kg) thrust General Electric F110-400 afterburning turbofans.
Dimensions: Span (68° sweep) 38ft 2in (11.63m), (20° sweep) 64ft 1½in (19.54m); length 62ft 8in (19.1m); height 16ft (4.88m); wing area (spread) 565ft² (52.49m²).
Weights: Empty 40,104lb (18,191kg); loaded (clean) 58,715lb (26,632kg), (max) 73,349lb (33,724kg).
Performance: Max speed 1,564mph (2,517km/h, Mach 2.34) at altitude, 910mph (1,470km/h, Mach 1.2) at sea level; initial climb rate (normal gross weight) over 30,000ft (9,144m)/min; service ceiling over 56,000ft (17,070m); range (fighter with external fuel) about 2,000 miles (3,200km).
Armament: One 20mm M61A-1 multibarrel cannon in fuselage; four AIM-7 Sparrow and four or eight AIM-9 Sidewinder air-to-air missiles, or up to six AIM-54 Phoenix and two AIM-9; max external weapon load in surface attack role 14,500lb (6,577kg).
History: First flight 21 December 1970; initial deployment with US Navy carriers October 1972, (F-14D) 1991.
Users: Iran, USA (Navy).

The F-14 has had a long career with virtually no major modification, and will remain in production until the 1990s with updates to the avionics and a new engine. Throughout its career the engine has been the only continual source of worry. The range and multiple-target capability of the radar and AAMs carried puts the aircraft in a class of its own.

Below: Though not part of the regular curriculum, the F-14A can carry an attack load of 14,500lb (6,577kg). This example is toting Snakeye retarded bombs, as well as a Sparrow and two Sidewinders.

Features include pilot and naval flight officer in unstaggered tandem Martin-Baker seats, a retractable refuelling probe on the right of the nose, widely spaced engines fed by fully variable inlet ducts, swing wings with pivots at the extremities of an almost flat upper surface of enormous area, main gears retracting forwards with the wheels rotating to lie in the fixed wing gloves, full-span powered leading-edge slats, trailing-edge flaps and roll-control spoilers (the latter augmented by the slab stabilators or horizontal tails), slightly canted twin vertical tails, and retractable canards called glove vanes which with increasing wing sweep pivot outwards.

The Hughes AWG-9 main radar has a 36in (0.914m) planar antenna and operates in many modes but usually in pulse/doppler to give a clear indication of airborne targets out to 195 miles (315km). It can track 24 targets while simultaneously engaging any selected six and guiding AAMs on to those targets.

The F-14 has been the only aircraft in service able to fire the AIM-54 Phoenix missile, also a Hughes product, which has demonstrated its ability to kill at ranges in excess of 125 miles (201km). Four of these large AAMs can be carried on special underfuselage pallets, and two more can be mounted on pylons under the wing gloves. Drop tanks, of 222gal (1,101l) capacity, can be hung under the engine ducts. The gun is mounted at the bottom of the left side of the fuselage, fed by a horizontal drum with 675 rounds.

By mid-1986 Grumman had delivered 530 F-14s, almost all of them F-14As. In 1987 production was to switch to the F110-powered F-14A Plus; two years later it will again change, to the F-14D, with new digital avionics, new cockpit displays, improved radar, ASPJ, JTIDS and the AIM-120A missile.

Grumman supplied 80 F-14As to Iran, where about half have fought in the war with Iraq (there have been unconfirmed reports of Tomcats operating together with F-4 Phantoms, the F-14s 'drawing in' Iraqi fighters like decoys, and the F-4s taking over for the kill). Support from the USA has been withheld, and Grumman's opinion is that Iran cannot use its AIM-54 missiles without support.

The rest of the F-14s serve with US Navy VFs 1, 2, 11, 14, 21, 24, 31, 32, 33, ▶

Below: Though very much a BVR (beyond visible range) killer, the Tomcat is no slouch in a dogfight, especially with automatic wing sweep. Here an Iranian F-14 is 'wrung out' prior to delivery.

▶ 41, 51, 74, 84, 101, 102, 103, 111, 114, 124, 142, 143, 154, 211 and 213. Two aircraft from VF-41, saw brief combat over the Gulf of Sidra on 19 August 1981 when they were attacked by two Libyan Su-22s. Both the latter were destroyed, by a Sidewinder AAM apiece, and the engagement merely confirmed the superior tactics of the Navy crews.

In close combat the F-14 is one of the few aircraft with an auto wingsweep programmer, to adjust wing angle continuously to the demands of Mach number and manoeuvres. F-14 missions are almost always governed by E-2C control aircraft, and comprise three basic CAP (combat air patrol) tasks, Forcap (cover for the task force), Barcap (barrier against an oncoming air attack), and Tarcap (target cover for friendly attack aircraft in hostile airspace).

Most F-14As have a chin fairing housing a FLIR, APN-154 radar beacon and ACLS (Automatic Carrier Landing System) antenna, but since 1982 Northrop has been supplying the TCS (TV Camera Set) as a replacement. This has a large forward-facing lens through which the crew can see a wide-angle TV picture of targets for acquisition, followed by a narrow magnified image for identification, at beyond visual distance. Another optional store is TARPS (Tactical Air Reconnaissance Pod System), normally carried on the right rear body pylon. This has a forward looking KS-87B frame camera, a KA-99 low altitude lateral oblique panoramic camera and AAD-5 IR linescan. So far 49 aircraft carry TARPS, and these serve as the Navy's interim reconnaissance aircraft.

Above: This aircraft of VF-41 Black Aces looks like picking up the first wire of its home carrier *Nimitz*. The photo was taken during Exercise 'Teamwork 80' off the Norwegian coast.

Below: Seen during the same exercise, another Black Aces aircraft lines up on the catapult, while aircraft 212 from VF-84 Jolly Rogers thunders into the sky, wings spread and with take-off flap setting.

IAI Kfir, Nesher (Dagger)

Origin: Israel Aircraft Industries Ltd, Israel.
Type: Multirole fighter and attack aircraft; (TC-2) trainer and EW aircraft.
Engine: (Except Nesher) One 17,900lb (8,119kg) General Electric J79-J1E afterburning turbojet. See text.
Dimensions: (Nesher) As Mirage 5; (Kfir) span 26ft 11½in (8.22m); length (C2) 51ft 4½in (15.65m), (C2 with Elta radar) 53ft 11½in (16.45m), (TC2) 54ft 1in (16.49m); height 14ft 11in (4.55m); wing area 374.6ft² (34.8m²), (foreplane) 17.87ft² (1.66m²).
Weights: (Kfir) Empty (C2, interceptor) 16,060lb (7,285kg); loaded (C2, half internal fuel plus two Shafrir) 20,700lb (9,390kg), (C2, max with full internal fuel, two tanks, seven 500lb/227kg bombs and two Shafrir) 32,340lb (14,670kg).
Performance: (C2) Max speed (clean) 863mph (1,389km/h) at sea level, over 1,516mph (2,440km/h, Mach 2.3) above 36,090ft (11,000m); initial climb rate 45,950ft (14,000m)/min; service ceiling 58,000ft (17,680m); combat radius (20min reserve, interceptor, two 110gal/500l tanks plus two Shafrir) 215 miles (346km), (attack, three 330gal/1,500l tanks plus seven bombs and two Shafrir, hi-lo-hi) 477 miles (768km).
Armament: Two IAI-built DEFA 5-52 guns each with 140 rounds; seven hardpoints for a total of 9,469lb (4,295kg) of various stores, always including two Shafrir 2 AAMs (outer wings) plus tanks, bombs (ten 500lb/227kg), Gabriel III, Maverick or Hobos missiles, rocket pods, Matra Durandal or other anti-runway weapons, napalm, ECM pods and tanks.
History: First flight (Nesher) reportedly September 1969, (Kfir prototype) 1972, (production) 1974, (C2) 1975, (TC2) February 1981, (C7) 1983.
Users: (Nesher) Argentina (named Dagger); (Kfir) Colombia, Ecuador, Israel, USA (Navy, Marine Corps).

The Nesher (Eagle) is a Mirage 5, powered by an Atar 9C but equipped with Israeli avionics. Substantial numbers were sold to Argentina, survivors from the Falklands War being equipped with inflight-refuelling probes, with IAI engineering support.

The Kfir (Lion Cub) is a redesigned aircraft with the J79 engine, enlarged ducts, a new engine bay of reduced length, a new dorsal fin with ram inlet, a revised cockpit, a new nose, a new fuel system, strengthened, longer-stroke main landing gears and avionics of Israeli origin. The first two aircraft were delivered in June 1975.

In the Kfir C2, small strakes along the sides of the nose and removable (but fixed-incidence) foreplanes above the inlets improved low-speed and combat-manoeuvre capability, which was further enhanced by extending the outer wing leading edge with a sharp dogtooth. The C2 has shorter take-off and landing run, a steeper landing approach in a flatter attitude and a reduced gust reponse in low-level attack.

The standard C2 has an extended nose housing the Elta EL/M-2001B ranging radar. Equipment includes inertial navigation, comprehensive flight-control and weapon-delivery systems and a high standard of EW/ECM installations. Further subsystems are in the rear cockpit of the two-seat TC2 version, first flown in 1981, with a down-sloping extended nose. The two-seater is used for conversion training in the two-pilot variant, and also as a dedicated EW aircraft.

In 1983 production switched to the Kfir C7, with an uprated engine, increased internal fuel, a new Hotas cockpit, increased gross weight, a digital computer for stores management, the WDNS 341 navigation and weapon-aiming system and, as an option, the big M-2021 pulse-doppler radar in place of the small ranging set.

IAI has delivered about 250 Kfirs, and offers update kits for users of the Mirage. The US Navy has borrowed 12 of the early Kfir (non-canard) fighters from Israel, with contract support by IAI, to try them out as 'hostile' opponents at NAS Oceana. Designated F-21A, they will be replaced by F-16Ns, but meanwhile a further 13 F-21As are being procured for use by the Marines at MCAS Yuma.

Below: Both Israel and the US Navy got a good deal with the three-year lease of a dozen early Kfirs as F-21A Aggressor aircraft, for use as 'MiG-simulators' during dissimilar air combat training at NAS Oceana. These C1s have very small canards and lack the wing dogtooth leading edge. The US Marines are also obtaining Kfirs.

IAI Lavi

Origin: Israel Aircraft Industries Ltd, Israel.
Type: Multirole aircraft with emphasis on surface attack.
Engine: One 20,620lb (9,353kg) thrust Pratt & Whitney PW1120 afterburning turbojet.
Dimensions: Span 28ft 9⅔in (8.78m); length 47ft 9½in (14.57m); height overall 15ft 8in (4.78m); wing area 355.75ft² (33.05m²).
Weights: (Provisional) Empty (equipped) 15,320lb (6,950kg); max (clean) 22,024lb (9,990kg), (external stores) 42,500lb (19,277kg).
Performance: Max speed (clean, hi-altitude) 1,221mph (1,964km/h, Mach 1.85), (lo, two 2,000lb Mk 84 bombs and two AAMs) 687mph (1,106km/h), (lo, eight 750lb M117 and two AAMs) 619 mph (997km/h); combat radius (lo, eight 750lb and two AAMs) 281 miles (452km), (hi-lo-hi, two Mk 84 or six Mk 82) 1,324 miles (2,131km).
Armament: Four underwing pylons for wide range of stores including bombs, Gabriel IIIAS or other missiles, rocket launchers, gun pods, ECM jammer pods and (inner pylons) drop tanks of up to 561gal (2,548l) capacity; six fuselage pylons for Mk 80 series bombs, to total external load of 16,000lb (7,258kg); wing-tip rails for AAMs such as Sidewinder, Shafrir 2 or Python 3.
History: First flight 31 December 1986; service delivery 1990.
Users: To include Israel.

Below: Taken during the first flight on the last day of 1986, this view shows that the first Lavi to be completed is a two-seater. The close kinship with the F-16 (apart from the canard) is obvious. The US Congress is exerting intense pressure to get the Lavi cancelled.

Far exceeding in effort and cost any previous aircraft project in Israel, the Lavi (Young Lion) is a totally IAI/Heyl Ha'Avir concept intended to replace the A-4 from 1990, and later the F-4 and Kfir. Though configured very much as a close-coupled air-combat aircraft, it is officially described as a 'single-seat close air support and interdiction aircraft, with secondary capability for air defence'. Another document goes even further, dismissing the defensive role entirely and wording the fighter aspect as 'air-to-air self-defence to and from the target'.

In fact the Lavi could hardly fail to be a superior air-combat aircraft, though it is unlikely to have much of an edge over Israel's existing F-16s. No mention has been made of an internal gun, and though an advanced pulse-doppler radar will be fitted this will not specifically be associated with long-range AAMs, but instead will have most operating modes tailored for interdiction.

Naturally IAI has had to rely on imported technology to a considerable degree in order to produce a state-of-the-art aircraft. So far every company named as participating in the programme is American, and this automatically weakens the project by giving the USA political control. This control has been strengthened by the State Department's refusal to grant licences for technology transfer, the US suppliers instead merely being allowed to export finished parts. This applies especially to the advanced composite airframe structures, which include the wing, canards, tail and movable surfaces. Grumman was picked as chief contractor for these items.

Overall, the programme has been very successful at the technical level, but less so on the political and financial front. By mid-1986 the USA had injected $1 billion into the programme, but an impasse then arose, caused by deep disputes over cost and the belief that the Lavi could take markets from US industry. Briefly, the US assessors disbelieved the Israeli estimates of a fly-away unit price of $13.5–15 million and insisted that the true figure could not be less than $22 million and might be much higher. In August 1986 US Defense ▶

▶ Secretary Weinberger ordered funding to be resumed, with an initial injection of a further $67 million, but also stipulated that Israel should consider 'several alternatives offered by the Pentagon'.

Of course, the Lavi is being designed to CCV principles, with an FBW flight control system, contractors for which include Lear-Siegler and Milco for the FBW avionics and Moog for the surface power units. Design load factor is 9g, and turn rates are to be 13.2°/sec sustained and 24.3°/sec instantaneous. Roll rate is to be 300°/sec. The external fuel is remarkable, 1,121gal (5,095l) compared with only 732gal (3,330l) internal. A typical attack load would comprise eight 1,000lb (454kg) cluster bomb units, two 600gal (2,727l) tanks on the outer pylons, and two self-defence AAMs on the wing tips.

Aerodynamically the Lavi follows today's preferred 'fighter' configuration, with close-coupled canards mounted above the root of a large delta wing. The latter has trailing-edge flaperons, but the leading-edge flaps extend only over the outer half of each wing and there is no dogtooth. The percentage of composite materials in the airframe, on a weight basis, is quite modest at 22 (compared with 30 for the Gripen, for example). All such parts for the first seven airframes are being supplied from the USA, these seven articles comprising a static-test specimen, four two-seat dual-control Lavis (one of which is the No 1 aircraft, which was flown on 31 December 1986) and two single-seaters. Should the Lavi be funded through to production, the transfer of many advanced technologies to Israel will be necessary. A special company, MMCA, has been formed to produce the graphite (carbon) epoxy composite parts. Bet-Shemesh Engines hopes eventually to produce most of the PW1120 powerplant under licence, but it appears unlikely that Israel has the industrial capacity to make all the advanced items needed for each aircraft.

Certainly the most crucial parts are the avionics, and here Israel is in a strong position. Elta is developing the multimode radar, derived from the M-2021B, with doppler beam sharpening, look-down and sea-search modes and automatic track-while-scan and target-acquisition in the air-to-air mode, using a programmable signal processor. Hughes is the prime contractor for the wide-angle holographic HUD, and Lear Siegler is underpinning MBT in developing the quadruplex-redundant digital FBW flight control system. Elbit Computers provide the cockpit display integration, one display being colour and two monochrome. The control stick is conventional. Elta is prime contractor for the very advanced electronic warfare subsystems, which include comprehensive threat detection and anaylsis, with an Elisra RWR (radar warning receiver), and extremely advanced active and passive countermeasures including computer-controlled power management for noise and deception jammers chaff and flare dispensers installed both internally and in external pods.

Israel hopes to build 300 Lavis at a rate of 24 per year. Squadron evaluation with 20 aircraft is due in 1991–92. Many hurdles remain to be crossed.

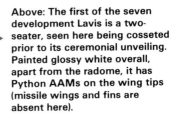

Above: The first of the seven development Lavis is a two-seater, seen here being cosseted prior to its ceremonial unveiling. Painted glossy white overall, apart from the radome, it has Python AAMs on the wing tips (missile wings and fins are absent here).

Left: This drawing gives a good idea of the appearance of the single-seat version, which is expected to make up the majority of the planned production run of 300. As this book went to press the programme was still under attack from various rival factions in the USA.

Lockheed F-19 (RF-19?)

Origin: Lockheed-California Company, USA.

Type: Covert reconnaissance and attack aircraft (data provisional).

Engines: Two 10,600lb (4,808kg) thrust General Electric F404-400 (Mod) turbofans.

Dimensions: Span 24ft 1½in (7.35m); length 50ft 2½in (15.3m); height 10ft 8½in (3.26m); wing area (with body) 710ft² (65.9m²).

Weights: Not disclosed, but maximum loaded is about 27,000lb (12,247kg).

Performance: Max speed (all heights) about 745mph (1,199km/h); combat radius, normally about 600 miles (966km).

Armament: Internal bay for precision attack weapons such as two AGM-65D Maverick or two Paveway III or similar 'smart' weapons.

History: First flight (XST) November 1977, (F-19A) 1982; combat service from before April 1984.

Users: USA (AF).

Most recent of the amazing 'cloak and dagger' aircraft programmes managed by Lockheed's Advanced Development Projects team at the famed 'Skunk Works', the F-19 is the end-product of one of the most fascinating design tasks ever faced. The objective, as stated by the DARPA (US Defense Advanced Research Projects Agency), was to create a 'low observables' aircraft, which could hardly be detected visually, nor by its sound, nor by its heat emission (IR, infrared), nor by existing radars or any other known sensor. To the public at large such aircraft are known under the general adjective of 'stealth'. The most remarkable feature of this pioneer stealth aircraft is that nobody tried to produce one 20 or 40 years ago.

Work began in a widespread research programme organized by USAF Aeronautical Systems Command and DARPA called 'Have Blue'. After experiments on a small Windecker Eagle, modified and given the designation YE-5, contracts were placed in 1975 and 1976 for the XST (Experimental Stealth Technology) aircraft, with minimal radar cross-section, noise and IR signature, and able to carry advanced 'spoofing' ECM. The contract for five prototypes was won by Lockheed, not least because of the proven record of the Skunk Works in handling programmes posing awesome challenges and the need for absolute secrecy. The ADP works is run by Ben Rich, but former boss 'Kelly' Johnson was brought back from retirement to serve as a consultant. The little XSTs were said to be 'bat like' and to resemble the Shuttle Orbiter, and the engines were reported as two General Electric J85 turbojets without afterburners. The five aircraft were conveyed from the Skunk Works in a C-5A and test flown at the so-called Ranch airstrip at Tonopah bombing range, adminstered by Nellis AFB, Nevada. The official name for the site is Groom Lake. In general the XSTs performed amazingly against all known sensors, though two were lost in crashes for reasons thought to be unconnected with stealth features.

In mid-1981 Lockheed won the big prize, the prime contract for the next-generation low-observables aircraft to be used by the USAF. Officially known as COSIRS, from Covert Survivable In-weather Reconnaissance Strike, the F-19A also had the project name Aurora. The name Specter has several times been applied, but so has the name Ghost; neither is confirmed as the official name.

In configuration the F-19A is naturally very like a scaled-up XST, but with new features. It has an internal weapons bay, attack sensors and full combat equipment, and to fit inside the C-5 transports its outer wings have power folding. Most other features were proven with the XST, including especially the overall configuration and the structural and coating materials. To save money parts of other aircraft were used where possible, the chief example of this being the F/A-18 main landing gears. The engines are also of F/A-18 type, but with the afterburners replaced by large and capacious jetpipes in which the hot jets are mixed with many times their own mass flow of cold fresh air to give a slow, cool and almost undetectable output jet whilst losing as little thrust as possible.

A kind of grossly modified tailless delta, the F-19A clearly has features in common with the very different SR-71 (another Skunk Works project), among them the shaping of the outer skin and internal structure to minimize the chance of any radar energy being sent back to its source. Almost the whole outer structure of the F-19A is carbon-fibre or Fiberloy boron-fibre material, finally painted with a ferrite-based coating containing billions of microscopic iron balls to generate currents which have a profound effect on radar reflectivity. Of course, the inlets are specially configured to eliminate radar reflectivity, and there are no flat surfaces or intersecting panels forming external angles. The fins mask the jetpipes, and the overall impression is one of extreme smoothness.

Most F-19As have a conventional cockpit and canopy, though experiments are in hand with the pilot inside a totally synthetic cockpit, needing no canopy at all, relying instead on TV and FLIR to 'see' the world outside. It is said that the aircraft is flown by an F-16 sidestick controller, and is exceedingly agile. Paint is all-grey, and so far no chameleon-like ability to change colour to match the background has been reported. A laser ranger is fitted under the nose, and there are comprehensive navigation and attack avionics, as well as various reconnaissance sensors.

All evidence indicates that the F-19A programme is large, with a three-figure total of aircraft. F-19As have been reported by English civilians from October 1985 onwards, some sightings surprisingly being of daytime approaches to RAF Binbrook. Other operations have been reported from Japan and Alaska. So far as one can tell, all F-19As are legitimate USAF aircraft, and the CIA has not been involved at all. Though equipped for attack missions, the prime task of the F-19A (an erroneous designation, denied by the US authorities) is clandestine reconnaissance, possibly at high or at very low levels where fuel burn permits.

Below: This model, made from a 1:48 scale Italeri plastic construction kit, gives a better idea of the general appearance of the F-19 (or it may be the RF-19, in view of its mission) than any of the artist's impressions previously published. In the author's view there is still room for some improvement, notably in the shape of the wing-tips and the size of the canted tails, but the overall configuration shows that this kit was not designed solely on the basis of pure guesswork!

McDonnell Douglas F-4 Phantom II

Origin: McDonnell Aircraft Company, USA; licensed to Mitsubishi, Japan.
Type: Originally carrier-based all-weather interceptor, now all-weather multirole fighter for ship or land operation; (F-4G) EW defence suppression aircraft; (RF) all-weather multisensor reconnaissance aircraft.
Engines: (C,D,RF) Two 17,000lb (7,711kg) General Electric J79-15 turbojets with afterburner; (E,F,G) 17,900lb (8,120kg) J79-17; (J,N,S) 17,900lb J79-10; (K,M) 20,515lb (9,305kg) Rolls-Royce Spey 202/203 augmented turbofans.
Dimensions: Span 38ft 5in (11.7m); length (C,D,J,N,S) 58ft 3in (17.76m), (E,G,F and all RF versions) 62ft 11in or 63ft (19.2m), (K,M) 57ft 7in (17.55m); height (all) 16ft 3in (4.96m); wing area 530ft² (49.2m²).
Weights: Empty (C,D,J,N) 28,000lb (12,700kg), (E,F, RF) 29,000lb (13,150kg), (G,K,M) 31,000lb (14,060kg); max (C,D,J,K,M,N,RF) 58,000lb (26,308kg), (E,G,F) 60,630lb (27,502kg).
Performance: Max speed with Sparrow missiles only (lo) 910mph (1,470km/h, Mach 1.2) with J79 engines, 920mph with Spey, (hi) 1,500mph (2,414km/h, Mach 2.27) with J79, 1,386mph with Spey; initial climb rate typically 28,000ft (8,534m)/min with J79, 32,000ft (9,750m)/min with Spey; service ceiling over 60,000ft (19,685m) with J79, 60,000ft with Spey; range (internal fuel, no weapons) about 1,750 miles (2,817km); ferry range (external fuel) typically 2,300 miles (3,700km), (E and variants) 2,600 miles (4,184km).
Armament: (All versions except RF models which have no armament) Four AIM-7 Sparrow or Sky Flash (later Amraam) air-to-air missiles recessed under fuselage; inner wing pylons can carry two more AIM-7 or four AIM-9 Sidewinder missiles; in addition E versions except RF have internal 20mm M61 multi-barrel gun, and virtually all versions can carry the same gun in external centreline pod; all except RF have centreline and four wing pylons for tanks, bombs or other stores to total weight of 16,000lb (7,257kg).
History: First flight (XF4H-1) 27 May 1958; service delivery (F-4A) February 1961 (inventory); first flight (Air Force F-4C) 27 May 1963, (F-4E) 30 June 1967, (F-4G) 1976.
Users: Egypt, West Germany, Greece, Iran, Israel, Japan, Saudi Arabia, South Korea, Spain, Turkey, UK (RAF), USA (AF, Navy, Marines, ANG).

Below: Taking off in full 'burner, this F-4E is based at Ramstein, West Germany, with the US Air Force's 86th TFW. It is very doubtful that the USAF will fund a PW1120 re-engining programme for any of its large number of surviving Phantoms.

Above: This F-4E, from the USAF's 3rd TFW, is normally based at Clark AB, Philippines. It is seen approaching a tanker (from which the photo was taken) with its refuelling receptacle open. Note the Westinghouse ALQ-119 ECM pod in the left forward missile bay.

By far the most important fighter in the non-Communist world during the past 20 years, the F-4 has an evergreen quality of sheer capability that from time to time is recognized. Egypt, for example, was about to sell its 34 F-4Es to Turkey but then realized this would leave them with no stand-off kill capability using radar-guided AAMs (a strange shortcoming of the otherwise much superior F-16) and the sale did not go through. Altogether 5,195 F-4s were built.

The original F-4A and F-4B for the US Navy introduced blown flaps and drooped leading edges, a broad fuselage with four radar-guided Sparrow AAMs recessed into the underside, wing and centreline pylons for tanks, Sidewinders, bombs or other stores, tremendous internal fuel capacity, tandem seats for pilot and RIO (radar intercept officer) and a big and powerful Westinghouse nose radar. This sub-family was continued via the F-4J of 1965 to today's F-4N and F-4S re-builds with more fuel, revised structures and avionics, slatted wings and tailplanes, and many other updates, which continue in service with the Navy and Marines.

The original USAF version was the F-4C of 1963, with minor changes to wheels and brakes, cockpits (usually configured for two pilots) and with an FR receptacle instead of a retractable probe. This proved so satisfactory that the Air Force was allowed to have its own F-4D, with ground attack avionics. This was followed during the Vietnam War by the F-4E with uprated engines, an extra rear-fuselage tank, a new and smaller radar, an M61 gun recessed under the nose and, in the course of the production run, powerful leading-edge slats instead of the blown droops, to improve the previously very poor agility when heavily laden with weapons near the ground.

The F-4E became the definitive fighter version, bought by several export customers, though West Germany's Luftwaffe chose a simpler F-4F model without provision for Sparrow medium-range AAMs or various EW subsystems. Mitsubishi assembled 138 F-4E(J) Phantoms in Japan, with increasing local content, the only Phantoms not built at St Louis. In 1964–65 Britain bought the F-4K (Phantom FG.1) for the Navy and F-4M (FGR.2) for the RAF. Both were redesigned with Spey engines, and this proved to be a very expensive mistake which at high altitude and high speed actually degraded the performance. In normal low-level use the big fan engines do a good job, and other features include, on the FGR.2, a Ferranti INS, AWG-11/12 radar fire control, a strike camera in one AAM recess and fin-cap RWR. ▶

Above: XV422 is one of the largely redesigned F-4M species, known to the RAF as the Phantom FGR.2. Painted in low-conspicuity grey, these Spey-engined aircraft have fin-cap radar warning receivers.

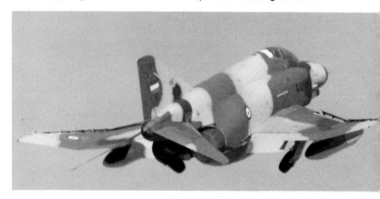

Above: Scramble by an F-4E of the Islamic Republic of Iran Air Force. Despite obvious problems, a fair number of the 227 aircraft supplied (F-4Ds, F-4Es and RF-4Es) continue to wage war against Iraq.

Below: Spain's Ejercito del Aire No 12 Wing at Torrejon received 40 F-4Cs (which are known in that service as C.12s) and four RF-4Cs.

Above: Two fully loaded F-4Es of the 86th TFW of USAF Europe, flying from Ramstein (and since re-equipped with F-16s). Each aircraft has four Sparrows, four Sidewinders and two tanks.

▶ Tornados are steadily replacing RAF Phantoms, but in the air-defence role Nos 111 and 43 Squadrons at Leuchars (FG.1), 29 at Coningsby and 56 at Wattisham are still operational, with 29 divided between Coningsby and RAF Mount Pleasant in the Falklands, the latter force being redesignated No 23 Sqn. To make up for the deployment of the Falklands aircraft 15 ex-USN fighters have been purchased at the high price of £125m and, after complete refurbishment at NAS North Island (San Diego), formed No 74 Sqn at Wattisham, where they are known as F-4J(UK).

The US Navy did not need a dedicated reconnaissance Phantom in the early 1960s, but the USAF quickly contracted for the RF-4C, which set a new standard in fighter-type aircraft used for multisensor reconnaissance without armament. It introduced a new nose, longer and slimmer, with no main radar but a small APQ-99 forward-looking radar and a main bay occupied by forward oblique, vertical and lateral oblique cameras. In the fuselage is an APQ-12 SLAR and an AAS-18A IR linescan. Various new communications include HF radio with a shunt aerial flush with the skin on each side of the fin. Ahead of the fin are two photoflash installations firing the cartridges upwards. The Marines bought RF-4Bs with similar equipment but also including cameras on rotating mountings, aimed by the pilot, and an inertial navigation system. Newest and best of the reconnaissance variants is the RF-4E, all built for export, based on the F-4E.

The latest Phantom is the F-4G Advanced Wild Weasel EW platform, its mission being to sense, locate and destroy hostile ground air-defence emitters. Used only by the USAF, this is a rebuild of late-model F-4E fighters with the APR-38 EW system whose 52 special aerials include large pods facing forwards under the nose and to the rear above the rudder. The system is governed by a Texas Instruments computer with reprogrammable software to keep up to date on all known hostile emitters. The aircraft carries such weapons as triplets of the AGM-65 EO-guided Maverick precision attack weapon, Shrike ARM (anti-radar missile) and HARM (high-speed ARM). Like almost all Phantoms, the left front fuselage recess often carries an ECM jammer pod (usually an ALQ-119), leaving the other three available for Sparrow AAMs if necessary; alternatively, Sidewinders can be carried under the wings.

In 1986 Germany's F-4Fs and Japan's F-4E(J)s were the subjects of major update programmes to fit look-down pulse-doppler radars. Meanwhile, Boeing and Pratt & Whitney have had a positive response to their joint proposal to re-engine as many F-4s as possible with the PW1120 powerplant (as used in the IAI Lavi). This programme is going ahead at IAI in Israel, and orders from other operators are being sought. Clearly, the F-4 Phantom will remain in service with a number of air arms for very many years yet.

McDonnell Douglas F-15 Eagle

Origin: McDonnell Aircraft Company, USA; assembled under licence by Mitsubishi, Japan.
Type: Air superiority fighter with attack capability; (TF) trainer; (E) dual-role fighter/attack aircraft.
Engines: Two 23,930lb (10,855kg) thrust Pratt & Whitney F100-100 afterburning turbofans; (E) two 23,450lb (10,640kg) F100-220.
Dimensions: Span 42ft 9¾in (13.05m); length 63ft 9in (19.43m); height overall 18ft 5½in (5.63m); wing area 608ft² (56.5m²).
Weights: Empty (A) 27,381lb (12,420kg); take-off (intercept mission, A) 42,206lb (19,145kg); max (A) 56,000lb (25,401kg), (C,FAST packs) 68,000lb (30,845kg), (E) 81,000lb (36,742kg).
Performance: Max speed (clean, over 45,000ft/13,716m) 1,650mph (2,655km/h, Mach 2.5), (clean, sea level) 910mph (1,470km/h, Mach 1.2); combat ceiling (A, clean) 63,000ft (19,200m); time to 50,000ft (15,240m) (intercept configuration) 2.5min; ferry range (C) over 3,450 miles (5,560km).
Armament: One 20mm M61A1 gun with 940 rounds; four AIM-7 Sparrow AAMs or eight AIM-120A (Amraam), plus four AIM-9 Sidewinders; three attack weapon stations (five with FAST packs) for external load of up to 16,000lb (7,258kg) or (E) 24,500lb (11,113kg).
History: First flight 27 July 1972; service delivery (inventory) November 1974; first flight (C) 26 February 1979, (E prototype) November 1982.
Users: Israel, Japan, Saudi Arabia, USA (AF, ANG).

Most observers in the Western World regard the F-15 as the natural successor to the F-4, and as the best fighter in the world. To a considerable degree its qualities rest on the giant fixed-geometry wing, F100 engine and Hughes APG-63 pulse-doppler radar.

Inevitably the F-15 emerged as a large aircraft. Two of the extremely powerful engines were needed to achieve the desired thrust/weight ratio, which near sea level in the clean condition exceeds unity. The lower edge of the fuselage is tailored to the snug fitting of four medium-range AAMs. The gun is in the bulged strake at the root of the right wing, drawing ammunition from a tank inboard of the duct. There is room in the integral-tank inner wing and between the ducts for 11,600lb (5,260kg, 1,448gal/6,592l) of fuel, and three 500gal (2,270l) drop tanks can be carried, each stressed to 5g manoeuvres

Below: First flight in June 1985 of USAF No 84-001, the first F-15C MSIP (Multi-Stage Improvement Program), with updated avionics.

when full. Roll is by ailerons only at low speeds, the dogtoothed slab tailplanes taking over entirely at speeds above Mach 1, together with the twin rudders, which are truly vertical.

Avionics are typical of the 1970 period, with a flat-plate-scanner pulse-doppler radar, a vertical situation display presenting ADI (attitude/direction indicator), radar and EO information in one picture, a HUD, an INS and a central digital computer. In its integral ECM/IFF subsystems the F-15 is better than most Western fighters, with Loral radar warning (with front/rear aerials on the left fin tip), a Northrop ALQ-135 internal countermeasures system, a Magnavox EW warning set and a Hazeltine APX-76 IFF with a Litton reply-evaluator. High-power jammers, however, must still be hung externally, Westinghouse pods normally occupying an outer pylon. The APG-63 offers an excellent capability in tracking low-level targets, with cockpit switches giving a Hotas (hands on throttle and stick) capability.

The original plan was to procure 729 F-15s, but this number has risen to 1,266, of which 1,010 had been delivered to the USAF and other customers by late 1986. Current production is centred on the F-15C and two-seat F-15D, which provide updates in mission capability. A programmable signal processor gives the ability to switch from one locked-on target to another, to switch between air and ground targets and to keep searching whilst already locked-on to one or more targets. An increase in memory capacity from 24 to 96K gives a new high-resolution radar mode which can pick one target from a large group at extreme range. Internal fuel is increased by 2,000lb (907kg) and conformal pallets, called FAST (Fuel and Sensor, Tactical) packs fit snugly on each side of the fuselage to increase total fuel by 9,750lb (4,422kg). ▶

Below: Israel uses the F-15A, B, C and D. Here three of the A version are seen flying over the historic hilltop fort of Masada.

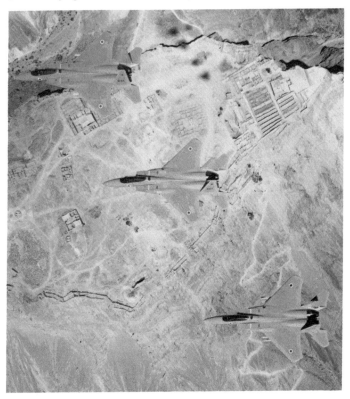

Above: Dive bombing from altitude would be suicidal in Europe, but this did not deter this demo by USAF 71-291, the F-15B used as the prototype F-15E.

Right: The Japanese Air Self-Defence Force is steadily becoming a major operator of the F-15, with licence-production of the F-15J. These four aircraft are from the 5th Training Wing, the first F-15J unit.

Above: This F-15C is one of 47 in service with the Royal Saudi Air Force, which also has 15 of the two-seat F-15D version. They replaced the venerable English Electric Lightning, vastly enhancing capability.

▶ In 1983 tangential carriage was introduced, enabling 12 bombs of 1,000lb (454kg), or four of twice this size, to be hung on short stub pylons along the lower edges of the FAST packs, giving reduced drag and leaving the existing pylons free (thus an F-15C can carry 12 bombs, four AAMs and two IR sensor pods, and still carry three tanks).

In the late 1970s the USAF began studying an ETC (Enhanced Tactical Fighter), configured equally for the surface attack and air superiority roles. McDonnell modified an early F-15B as the Enhanced Eagle, and after prolonged tests this carried the day over the rival F-16XL, though the resulting F-15Es will comprise 392 aircraft already in the programme. It will stick with the F100 engine, but in an improved Dash-220 form. A tandem-seater, the F-15E will have the new APG-70 high-resolution radar, with DBS (doppler beam sharpening), a totally new computer and programmable armament control system, a wide-field HUD, an internal ASPJ ECM, LANTIRN all-weather nav/targeting pods, and multifunction displays in the rear cockpit for managing the complete mission.

Under a $118 million contract McDonnell is modifying an F-15 with canard foreplanes, part-vectoring engine nozzles of 2D (two-dimensional) form and other changes. It is intended to have enhanced manoeuvrability and to operate from runways 'shorter than 1,500ft (457m)'.

McDonnell Douglas F/A-18 Hornet

Origin: McDonnell Douglas Corporation, with Northrop associate contractor, USA; RAAF aircraft assembled by GAF, Australia.

Type: Carrier- or land-based fighter and attack aircraft; (TF) dual trainer; (R) reconnaissance aircraft.

Engines: Two General Electric F404-400 afterburning turbofans, each 'in 16,000lb (7,258kg) thrust class'.

Dimensions: Span (with missiles) 40ft 4¾in (12.31m), (without missiles) 37ft 6in (11.42m); length 56ft (17.07m); height 15ft 3½in (4.66m); wing area 400ft² (36.16m²).

Weights: (Provisional) Empty 20,583lb (9,336kg); loaded (clean) 33,642lb (15,260kg), loaded (attack mission) 49,200lb (22,317kg); max loaded (catapult limit) 50,064lb (22,710kg).

Performance: Max speed (clean, at altitude) 1,190mph (1,915km/h, Mach 1.8), (max weight, sea level) subsonic; sustained combat manoeuvre ceiling, over 49,000ft (14,935m); combat radius (air-to-air mission, hi, no external fuel) 461 miles (741km); ferry range over 2,300 miles (3,700km).

Armament: One 20mm M61 gun with 570 rounds in upper part of forward fuselage; nine external weapon stations for max load (catapult launch) of 13,400lb (6,080kg) or (land take-off) of 17,000lb (7,711kg), including bombs, sensor pods, missiles (including Sparrow) and other stores, with wing-tip Sidewinders.

History: First flight (YF-17) 9 June 1974, (first of 11 test F-18s) 18 November 1978, (production F/A-18) 1980; service entry 1982.

Users: Australia, Canada, Spain, USA (Navy, Marine Corps). ▶

Above: A Sidewinder being fired from a Hornet of Marine squadron VMFA-314 Black Knights, from El Toro and USS *Coral Sea*.

Below: CF-188s of the Canadian Armed Forces, with two-seaters nearest the camera. As the name Hornet is not bilingual (English and French) it is not used in Canadian service.

▶ From the outset in 1974 the Hornet was designed to be equally good in both fighter and attack roles, replacing the F-4 in the first and the A-7 in the second. Though not a large aircraft, with dimensions between those of the compact Tornado and the F-4, and significantly smaller than the F-15, the F-18 combines the Tornado's advantage of small afterburning engines and large internal fuel capacity with avionics and weapons configured from the start for both F and A missions. Of course, in the low-level attack role its wide-span fixed wing gives severe gust response, and the Hornet suffers from a relatively low maximum speed and a lack of terrain-following radar. In weapon carriage the Hornet is first class with plenty of pylons and payload capability, and unlike its most immediate rival, the F-16, it has from the start carried a high-power liquid-cooled radar, the Hughes APG-65, matched with radar-guided AAMs.

It would be easy to criticize the armament as the only old part of a new aircraft, but in fact the M61 gun is still hard to beat, and the AIM-7 Sparrow and -9 Sidewinder AAMs have been so updated over the years that both remain competitive. In most air-combat situations the Hornet can hold its own, and compared with previous offensive (attack) aircraft it is in a different class; it is in the long-range interdiction role that Hornet has significant shortcomings.

These centre chiefly on radius with a given weapon load, though it has been pointed out this can be rectified to some extent by using larger external tanks and by air refuelling, the aircraft being equipped with a retractable probe in the upper right side of the nose. Forward vision is good, and the cockpit will always be a major 'plus' for this aircraft, with Hotas controls (the stick being

Below: VMFA-314 get the publicity again, this time embarked aboard USS _Coral Sea_ as part of Carrier Air Group CVW-13. Purple-jacketed fuelling crews are at work on two of the three aircraft being readied for a mission. Note the soot stains round the gun muzzles.

conventional instead of a sidestick), up-front CNI controls and three excellent MFDs (multifunction displays) which replace virtually all the traditional instruments. This cockpit goes further than anything previously achieved in enabling one man to handle the whole of a defensive or an offensive mission — but this is not to deny that a second crew member would not ease the workload.

There is, of course, a two-seat dual-pilot version for conversion training; this retains the weapons capability and the APG-65 radar, but has about 6 per cent less internal fuel. There is also a prototype of a dedicated reconnaissance F/A-18(R), testing of which began in August 1984. This has a new nose, with the gun and ammunition replaced by a reconnaissance package which would normally include optical cameras and/or AAD-5 IR linescan. It is stated that this model could 'overnight' be converted into the fighter/attack configuration.

The first Navy/Marines training squadron, VFA-125, commissioned at NAS Lemoore in November 1980. Three Marine Corps squadrons, VMFA-314, -323 and -531, were equipped by mid-1984, with three others following, while Navy squadrons are now also converting at lower priority. Until 1984 the Hornet was cleared operationally only for the fighter mission, because the Marines needed to replace the F-4 in this role more urgently. The attack mission depends to some degree on adding the laser spot tracker and FLIR.

In 1984 a structural problem surfaced — cracking of the tips of the fins and the fin/fuselage attachment. As an interim measure, the angle of attack was limited to 25° below 30,000ft when the aircraft was flying at between 300 and 400kts. Modification kits were installed in the field, while modified fins entered production later that year.

The Canadian CF-188 differs in small items such as having a spotlight for the visual identification of aircraft at night. Canada has only a small manufacturing offset (Canadair makes nose sections), despite the size of the order — 138 aircraft, including 24 TF-18s. Deliveries began in October 1982, the first unit to convert being No 410, followed by 490, 416 and 425 Sqns previously equipped with the CF-101, 439 in the Canadian Air Group at Baden-Söllingen, and then the Group's other squadrons, 421 and 441, previously CF-104 units.

Australia's buy of 57, plus 18 TFs, has triggered a vast and complex involvement of local industry. The first two TFs were delivered from St Louis in May 1985, and the rest are being assembled by Government Aircraft Factories, with major Australian content, to re-equip Nos 3, 75 and 77 Sqns. Australian offsets are 25 per cent. Spain, however, has bought 72 (plus 12 options) EF-18s, for $3,000 million, with offsets of $1,800 million, including local manufacture of various movable surfaces, panels and pylons.

Below: Predictably, Australia ran into sizeable problems with its massive and deeply complex offset programme, but aircraft are flowing to the RAAF nevertheless. This was the first two-seater, which was completed at St Louis. The RAAF is also building new Hornet bases.

McDonnell Douglas/BAe AV-8B Harrier II

Origin: McDonnell Douglas Corporation USA (prime contractor) and British Aerospace, UK.
Type: Multirole close-support attack aircraft.
Engine: One 21,700lb (9,843kg) thrust Rolls-Royce F402-406 Pegasus vectored-thrust turbofan.
Dimensions: Span 30ft 4in (9.25m); length 46ft 4in (14.12m); height 11ft 8in (3.55m); wing area 230ft² (21.37m²).
Weights: Basic operating 13,086lb (5,936kg); max (VTO) 19,185lb (8,702kg), (STO) 31,000lb (14,061kg).
Performance: Max speed (clean, sea level) 647mph (1,041km/h); dive Mach limit 0.93; combat radius (STO, seven Mk 82 bombs plus tanks, lo profile, no loiter) 748 miles (1,204km); ferry range 2,879 miles (4,633km).
Armament: Seven external pylons, centreline rated at 1,000lb (454kg) inboard wing 2,000lb (907kg), centre wing 1,000lb (454kg) and outboard 630lb (286kg), for total external load of 7,000lb (3,175kg) for VTO or 17,000lb (7,711kg) for STO; in addition ventral gun pods for one 25mm GAU-12/U gun and 300 rounds.
History: First flight (YAV-8B rebuild) 9 November 1978, (AV-8B) November 1981, (TAV-8B) 23 October 1986; service entry 1983.
Users: USA (Marine Corps), Spain (Navy).

Though developed directly from the original British Aerospace Harrier, the Harrier II is a totally new aircraft showing quite remarkable improvement and refinement in almost every part. This is especially the case in the radius of action with any given weapon load, but it also extends to the scope and variety of possible loads, and to the general comfort and pleasure of flying. The development was undertaken for the US Marine Corps and RAF, the latter's GR.5 version being the next entry in this book.

The original Harrier required a lot of attention, especially during accelerating or decelerating transitions, and suffered from a poor all-round view and a distinctly traditional cockpit, whereas the Harrier II offers a completely new environment which makes full use of the experience gained with the F-15 and F-18. At the same time, apart from the wing, which is a completely new long-span structure made almost entirely from graphite composites, the new aircraft is a joint effort with inputs from both partners.

The wing is the most obvious visible difference, compared with earlier Harriers. Apart from giving vastly greater lift, at the expense of extra drag, it houses much more fuel, so that total internal fuel capacity is 50 per cent greater. With eight sinewave spars and composite construction it is virtually unbreakable, with essentially limitless fatigue life, and the curved Lerx (leading-edge root extensions) greatly enhance combat manoeuvrability. ▶

Below: From this angle there is obvious close kinship between the AV-8B Harrier II, nearest camera, and the earlier AV-8A in the rear. Apart from the new wing the most apparent difference is the bigger nose and raised, bulged canopy.

▶ Under the wing are six stores pylons, four of them plumbed for tanks which are normally of 250gal (1,136l) size. The underfuselage gun pods are specially configured to serve as LIDS (lift-improvement devices) which, joined across the front by a retractable dam, provide a cushion of high-pressure air under the aircraft which counters the suck-down effect of rising air columns around the fuselage. In the AV-8B a 25mm gun is housed in the left pod with its ammunition fed from the right pod.

In the matter of avionics and EW the Harrier II is dramatically updated, the basic kit including INS (Litton ASN-130A), digital air-data and weapons computers, a large field of view HUD, fibre-optic data highways and comprehensive RWR and ECM systems. The primary weapon-delivery system is the Hughes ARBS (Angle Rate Bombing System), with dual-wavelength TV/laser target acquisition and tracking.

The one major avionics deficiency has always been the lack of a radar. McDonnell Douglas has a contract to study, and later flight-test, a multimode radar, which might incur a penalty of only 119lb (54kg). This could become standard by 1988, and be retroffitted. Slightly later in timing is a FLIR-based night attack system, which is to be fitted on Marines and also RAF Harrier IIs by 1990. A third update would be an uprated engine, derived from the XG-15 in which thrust is increased by some 3,000lb (1,361kg) while also improving engine life and maintainability.

The Marine Corps are receiving 300 AV-8Bs and 28 TAV-8B trainers with tandem staggered cockpits, a taller vertical tail and limited weapons capability. The first export customer is the Spanish Navy, which is receiving 12 US-assembled EAV-8Bs to equip a new squadron aboard the carrier *Principe de Asturias*.

Left: 'KD' tail codes identify this formation as from the training squadron, VMAT-203, from MCAS Cherry Point. Each aircraft has all six wing pylons installed, and the training syllabus includes various types of air firing and weapon delivery.

Below left: An AV-8 of the US Marine Corps makes a rolling (non-catapult) take-off from the level (non-ski ramp) deck of an amphibious warfare ship. Nozzles are quickly rotated to about the 55° setting just before the edge of the deck is reached.

Below: From some angles the Harrier II's wing, arching up in a hump-back over the fuselage, gives the aircraft an appearance resembling a giant vulture. Here seen on a paved strip, the AV-8B has demonstrated that it can operate from short stretches of reasonably firm, flat ground. In the author's view this is the only way to survive in war.

McDonnell Douglas/BAe Harrier GR.5

Origin: McDonnell Douglas, USA, and British Aerospace, UK (the latter in this case being prime contractor).

Type: Multirole close support and reconnaissance aircraft.

Engine: One 21,750lb (9,866kg) Rolls-Royce Pegasus 105 vectored-thrust turbofan.

Dimensions: Span 30ft 4in (9.25m); length 46ft 4in (14.12m); height 11ft 8in (3.55m); wing area (excluding LERX) 230ft² (21.37m²).

Weights: Basic operating 13,798lb (6,258kg); loaded (VTO) 18,950lb (8,595kg); normal operating 31,000lb (14,061kg).

Performance: Max speed (sea level) 647mph (1,041km/h), (hi altitude) 602mph (968km/h, Mach 0.91); combat radius (lo, 12 Mk 82 bombs, 1hr loiter, no external fuel) 103 miles (167km); ferry range 2,441 miles (3,929km).

Armament: Two 25mm Aden cannon, each with 200 rounds; in addition, 9,200lb (4,173kg) of external stores can be carried on nine pylons, with individual stores up to 2,000lb (907kg) including AIM-9L Sidewinder missiles for self-defence.

History: First flight 30 April 1985; service delivery late 1986.

User: UK (RAF).

As described on the preceding pages, the Harrier II is a complete revision of the original Harrier, developed jointly by the McDonnell Aircraft Company and British Aerospace at Kingston. The primary customer, who has taken the first 70 or so production aircraft, is the US Marine Corps, with aircraft assembled at St Louis. The RAF has purchased similar machines, designated Harrier GR.5, assembled at Kingston/Dunsfold, to a later time schedule. As this book went to press there was some confusion over the number to be built. UK defence cuts were announced in July 1986, when it was stated that the

number of GR.5s to be purchased might be reduced. Two weeks later it was announced that British Aerospace, the prime contractor for this version, had been authorized to provide long-lead items (i.e. parts taking a long time to make) for a further 18 aircraft on top of the original orders of two development prototypes and 60 for the inventory, and that McDonnell Douglas was further being asked for an additional nine sets. thus the total is likely to be 89, of which 87 are for squadron service in RAF Germany.

Compared with the USMC AV-8B there are numerous changes. The gun armament comprises two separate cannon, each with its own magazine in a self-contained pod, and ahead of the outrigger landing gears are extra pylons for self-defence Sidewinder AAMs. The engines have DSIC FADEC (full-authority digital engine control), giving enhanced performance and longer life.

The GR.5 is to differ in many avionics items, though the RWR will have its forward-looking receivers in the wing tips as on the AV-8B rather than in a fin-tip fairing as in early Harriers. The RAF may use a different chaff/flare payload dispenser, though it will be installed in the same bay behind the airbrake. The AV-8B is likely to carry the ALQ-164 jammer pod on the centreline pylon. Both variants will have a bolt-on FR probe pack, added above the left inlet duct, the probe being extended hydraulically when required.

The GR.5s will have Martin-Baker Mk 12 seats, stronger leading edges, nose and windshield to meet a severe bird-strike requirement, and considerable internal mission equipment including Marconi/Northrop Zeus active ECM and BAe Dynamics MIRLS (miniature IR linescan), both of which result in small fuselage blister fairings. Another non-standard feature is the Ferranti moving-map display, quite separate from the single MFD (multifunction display) similar to those in the F-18. The RAF will have no difficulty converting pilots on the existing Harrier T.4s, supplemented by simulator training.

Below: Though having very high commonality with the AV-8B, the Harrier GR.5 differs in many details, the most prominent being the additional Sidewinder pylons ahead of the outrigger landing gears. Ventral strakes replace the 25mm guns which are not yet quite ready.

MiG-21, J-7 (Fishbed, Mongol)

Origin: The OKB named for Mikoyan/Guryevich, Soviet Union; licensed to Hindustan Aeronautics Ltd, India; (J-7) Chinese State factory at Xian.
Type: (Most) Fighter; (some) fighter/bomber or reconnaissance aircraft.
Engine: (21) One 11,243lb (5,100kg) Tumanskii R-11 afterburning turbojet, (21F) 12,677lb (5,750kg) R-11F, (21PF) 13,120lb (5,950kg) R-11F2, (21FL, PFS, PFM, US) 13,668lb (6,200kg) R-11-300, (PFMA, M, R) R-11F2S-300, same rating, (MF,RF,SMT,UM, early 21bis) 14,550lb (6,600kg) R-13-300, (21bis) 16,535lb (7,500kg) R-25.
Dimensions: Span 23ft 5½in (7.15m); length almost all versions, including instrumentation boom) 51ft 8½in (15.76m), (excluding boom and inlet centrebody) 44ft 2in (13.46m); height overall (typical) 13ft 5½in (4.1m); wing area 247.57ft² (23m²).
Weights: Empty (F) 10,979lb (4,980kg), (MF) about 12,300lb (5,580kg), (bis) 12,600lb (5,715kg); loaded (typical, half internal fuel and two K-13A) 15,000lb (6,800kg), (full internal fuel and four K-13A) 18,078lb (8,200kg); max (bis, two K-13A and three drop tanks) 23,148lb (10,500kg).
Performance: Max speed (typical of all, sea level) 800mph (1,290km/h, Mach 1.05), (36,000ft/11,000m, clean) 1,385mph (2,230km/h, Mach 2.1); initial climb rate (F) about 30,000ft (9,144m)/min, (bis) 58,000ft (17,680m)/min; service ceiling (bis, max) 59,055ft (18,000m); practical ceiling (all) rarely above 50,000ft (15,240m); range with internal fuel (F) 395 miles (635km), (bis) 683 miles (1,100km); max range with three tanks (bis) 1,237 miles (1,992km).
Armament: (21F) One (rarely two) NR-30 guns, two pylons for K-13A AAMs or UV-16-57 rockets, (FL and all subsequent) one GP-9 belly pack containing GSh-23L gun with 200 rounds, or same gun mounted internally, and four wing pylons for K-13A, R-60 or (possibly) AS-7 missiles, or up to 3,307lb (1,500kg) other loads including bombs, rockets or two 108gal (490l) drop tanks. HAL-built aircraft carry Magic AAMs, J-7s CAA-1 and -2 AAMs.

Below: Trestles and jacks suggest that this MiG-21MF of the East German LSK (Air Force) is having at least a tyre change. To change an engine the whole rear fuselage and tail is removed; this used to be a common procedure with fighters.

Above: When India and Pakistan erupted into war in December 1971 the Hindustan-built Type 77 (MiG-21FL) was deployed in natural metal and also with several kinds of locally applied camouflage, using mainly green and brown paints. Armament comprised two K-13A ('Atoll') missiles and the GP-9 gun pack.

Above: Take-off by a Hindustan Type 76 (based on the MiG-21PFL) of the Indian AF. Similar aircraft have flown more than four million hours, but the basic design is now becoming so dated that these famous tailed deltas are passing to the scrap heap.

History: First flight (Ye-50) November 1955, (Ye-6) 1957; service delivery (21) 1959.
Users: (MiG-21) Afghanistan, Algeria, Angola, Bangladesh, Bulgaria, Cuba, Czechoslovakia, Egypt, Ethiopia, Finland, East Germany, Hungary, India (and HAL-built), Indonesia, Iraq, North Korea, Laos, Malagasy, Mozambique, Nicaragua, Nigeria, Peru, Poland, Romania, Somalia, Soviet Union, Sudan, Syria, Uganda, Vietnam, Yemen Arab Rep., Yemen People's Rep., Yugoslavia, Zambia; (J-7) Albania, China, Egypt, Iraq, Tanzania, Zimbabwe.

Several thousand MiG-21s of many versions remain in service with 38 air forces. All are small tailed-delta fighters with a generally rather limited capability.

By 1960 the PF variant, with a larger engine inlet than earlier models, providing room for an RIL ('Spin Scan') radar, was in production. The dorsal spine ▶

Right: Seen during a courtesy visit to Swedish and French fighter bases in 1978, this pristine MiG-21bis has the individual aircraft number (within its Kubinka-based regiment) of 40, as well as a special slogan celebrating the 17th Congress of the Leninist Young Communist League of the Soviet Union. Apart from the recessed GSh-23L gun it is unarmed, but it carried drop tanks throughout the Western visit. Though there are gross differences between some members of the MiG-21 family, the later variants are often remarkable look-alikes and the important differences in engine type, fuel capacity, avionic systems and other variables do not show externally except to a real expert. Perhaps the hardest versions to tell apart are the most numerous, the MiG-21MF and MiG-21bis.

▶ was enlarged to raise internal fuel to 616gal (2,800l), the gun(s) were removed, the main tyres were increased in size (causing bulges above and below the wing root), the instrument boom was moved to the top of the nose, and the avionics were changed and upgraded. By 1961 PF and PFL variants had introduced a further broadened fin (twice the area of the original), a drag-chute compartment at the base of the rudder, small lips above and below the jet nozzle, and provision for ATO (assisted take-off) rockets.

Most aircraft by late 1961 had a conventional side-hinged canopy with fixed screen and blown flaps which reduced the landing speed and the required field length. By 1965 the PFS and PFM had introduced the F2S-300 engine, more powerful R2L radar and the GP-9 gunpack. The MiG-21PFMA has 'Jay Bird' radar, four pylons and an enlarged dorsal spine giving a straight line from canopy to fin.

Up to this point all models also had tandem dual trainer versions (NATO name 'Mongol'), though most MiG-21U trainers are based on early series. Chinese production has been of early 66-series 21Fs, though in 1986 the upgraded F-7M Airguard was available for export.

By 1968 basic Soviet production featured over 20 different fits of EW equipment, reconnaissance cameras and flash cartridges, some aircraft being dedicated 21R and RF reconnaissance versions with pods which include SLAR. By far the most numerous models are the MF fighter-bomber, the SMB with a giant dorsal tank spine, and the MiG-21bis with the R-25 engine and further improved avionics.

Left: The JRV (Yugoslav Air Force) has an estimated 200 MiG-21s of five sub-types. Looking particularly well kept, this PFM may just have had an overhaul. This model is, in Yugoslavia, often fitted with the GP-9 gun pack, housing a GSh-23L cannon and 200 rounds of 23mm ammunition, but it is absent from this particular aircraft. The PFM was the first version of the MiG-21 to have a fixed windscreen and a cockpit canopy which hinged open to the right.

Below: Large numbers have been built of the MiG-21U, US and UM tandem dual-control trainers, which have the NATO name Mongol. Most have a periscope to give the instructor a better view ahead during landing. Here a MiG-21US of the LSK is serviced, and the oxygen bottles in the mainwheel bay replenished.

MiG-23 (Flogger)

Origin: The OKB named for Mikoyan/Guryevich, Soviet Union.
Type: (Most) Multirole fighter and attack aircraft; (U) operational trainer.
Engine: (Most) One 27,560lb (12,500kg) thrust Tumanskii R-29 afterburning turbojet, (S, SM and U) 22,485lb (10,200kg) Tumanskii R-27.
Dimensions: Span (72° sweep) 26ft 9⅔in (8.17m), (16°) 46ft 9in (14.25m); length (most, exc probe) 55ft 1½in (16.8m); height overall 14ft 4in (4.35m); wing area (16°) 293.4ft² (27.26m²).
Weights: Empty (MF) 24,250lb (11,000kg); loaded (clean, MF) 34,390lb (15,600kg); max (BM, two tanks and six FAB-500) 44,312lb (20,100kg).
Performance: Max speed (hi, clean, MF) 1,553mph (2,500km/h, Mach 2.35), (sea level, clean, MF) 910mph (1,470km/h, Mach 1.2); service ceiling (MF) 61,000ft (18,600m); take-off run 2,950ft (900m); combat radius (MF, fighter mission) 560–805 miles (900–1,300km).
Armament: (23MF interceptor) One 23mm GSh-23L gun with 200 rounds, two R-23R (AA-7 'Apex') and four R-60 (AA-8 'Aphid') AAMs.
History: First flight (Ye-231) probably 1966; service entry (23S) 1971.
Users: (MF) Czechoslovakia, East Germany, Hungary, North Korea, Poland, Romania, Soviet Union; (BM and other export models) Algeria, Bulgaria, Cuba, Egypt, Ethiopia, India, Iraq, North Korea, Libya, Sudan, Syria, Vietnam.

Built at a higher rate than any other combat aircraft throughout each of the past ten years, the MiG-23 and -27 (*qv*) together constitute the most important single type in the WP air forces, and are also being exported in substantial quantities.

The basic design has the same aerodynamics as the Su-24, but the aircraft is smaller and half as powerful. The VG wing, which appears to have gone out of fashion with Western nations, gives great lift for take-off and loiter with heavy loads of fuel and weapons, and in the MiG-23MF interceptor roughly doubles the patrol endurance to a maximum of almost 4hr. With the wings at 72° supersonic drag is greatly reduced and the aircraft is ideally configured for either an air-to-air interception with stand-off kill by missiles or for a lo attack on a surface target.

All versions have more or less the same airframe, designed to a load factor of 8g and for operation from rough airstrips. The first production series was

the MiG-23MF, in various sub-types called 'Flogger-B' by NATO. This usually carries the J-band radar called 'High Lark', with a large nose radome carrying a downward-sloping pitot boom at its tip; yaw and angle of attack sensors are on the forward fuselage together with doppler radar, IFF, ILS and, in a ventral fairing, an IR sensor. Standard Sirena 3 radar warning is fitted, together with comprehensive ECM threat-analysis and jamming, though for penetrating high-threat areas jammer/flare/chaff dispensers must occupy at least one pylon. The radar was likened by the USA to that of the F-4J and described as ▶

Above: An early production MiG-23M (one of several models called 'Flogger-B' by NATO). Wings are fully swept, which can save space on the flight-line.

Left: Taken at Tripoli in 1975, this was one of the first good MiG-23 photographs to reach the West. It shows the export vesion (NATO 'Flogger-E'), which has a lower standard of equipment and a smaller and less versatile radar. Since that time the Libyan national marking has been changed to plain Islamic green.

▶ the first Soviet type to have a significant capability against low-level targets; later the 23MF demonstrated an impressive ability to engage targets at far above its own altitude using the large R-23R missile.

The trainer version has a substantially redesigned forward fuselage with a slimmer nose housing R2L-series radar, two stepped cockpits with separate hinged canopies, a periscope for the instructor at the rear and a sloping sill extending to the front of the windscreen, and a larger dorsal spine fairing covering the much larger air-conditioning system. Internal fuel is naturally reduced, and the engine is the R-27. No M-series NATO name has been assigned.

A variant of the MF, called 'Flogger-G', has a smaller dorsal fin and has been seen with a new undernose sensor pod.

Right: Sometimes derided by Western writers for alleged poor power of manoeuvre, the MiG-23 family have not given this impression to those who have seen one demonstrated. This MiG-23MF ('Flogger-G') was doing a show for the Swedish Air Force, and is seen in full afterburner, pulling g (note vapour condensation over the wing gloves; at other times during this display the whole upper wing surface was enveloped in condensation).

Below: These MiG-23MF ('Flogger-G') interceptors appear to lack the infra-red seeker normally mounted in a chisel blister under the nose. They do, however, have the body missile pylons and the recessed GSh-23L gun under the fuselage. Further pylons can be attached under the fixed wing gloves and also under the swivelling outer wings, the latter pylons being used only with wings at the minimum sweep angle (they are generally used for ferry auxiliary fuel tanks).

MiG-25 (Foxbat)

Origin: The OKB named for Mikoyan/Guryevich, Soviet Union.
Type: High-altitude interceptor; (R) multisensor reconnaissance and elint aircraft; (U) trainer.
Engines: (Most) Two 27,120lb (12,300kg) thrust Tumanskii R-31 afterburning turbojets, (M) two 30,865lb (14,000kg) R-31F.
Dimensions: Span 45ft 9in (13.95m), (25R) 44ft (13.4m); length 73ft 2in (22.3m); height 18ft 4½ in (5.6m); wing area (gross) 611.7ft² (56.83m²), (25R) 603ft² (56m²).
Weights: (Typical) Empty equipped (25) just over 44,090lb (20,000kg), (25R) 43,200lb (19,600kg); max loaded (25) 79,800lb (36,200kg), (25R) 73,635lb (33,400kg).
Performance: Max speed (36,000ft/11,000m and above, 4 AAMs) 1,850mph (2,987km/h, Mach 2.8); max climb rate 40,950ft (12,480m)/min; service ceiling (25) 80,000ft (24,400m), (both 25R versions) 88,580ft (27,000m), combat radius (all) 710 miles (1,130km).
Armament: Four wing pylons each equipped to launch either version of AA-6 'Acrid' AAM (usually two radar, two IR); alternatively various combinations of AA-6, R-23R (AA-7) and R-60 (AA-8); (R) none seen; (U) recent photographs show missile pylons.
History: First flight (Ye-26) 1964, (production MiG-25) 1969; service delivery (25 and 25R) 1970.
Users: (25) Algeria, Libya, Soviet Union, Syria; (R) Algeria, India, Libya, Soviet Union, Syria; (U) India, Libya, Soviet Union; (M) Soviet Union.

The fastest combat aircraft ever put into service, the MiG-25 was originally designed to intercept the USAF RS-70 Valkyrie (which was cancelled). Speed and agility being incompatible, the MiG-25 is a 'straight line' aircraft. It takes time to work up to full speed, burning fuel at a prodigious rate, and once at Mach 2.8 (the limit with AAMs) the aircraft has a turn radius of many miles.

The wing is tapered on the leading edge and set at 4° anhedral. The slim fuselage merges into giant flanking air ducts with doors above and below, large bleed outlets, a variable roof profile and variable transverse control shutters. About 3,850gal (17,500l) of special T-6 fuel is housed in nine welded-steel tanks. The basic airframe material is steel, with leading edges of titanium.

The only movable surfaces comprise powered ailerons well inboard, powered slab tailplanes, twin powered rudders and plain flaps (apparently not blown). Twin ventral fins incorporate tail bumpers, with an airbrake between them, and twin braking parachutes can be streamed from the rear of the dorsal spine. The landing gears have high-pressure tyres.

The original radar, called 'Fox Fire' by NATO, was a typical 1959 set, of great size and weight and using vacuum tubes. Its rated output of 600kW was used to burn through hostile jamming, but even the earliest MiG-25 interceptors were well equipped with EW systems. CW illuminating transmitters occupy the front of each wing-tip fairing in this version.

Apart from the uprated engne, the 25M ('Foxbat-E') has a completely new radar and many other avionics improvements, though full details are not yet known. The airframe is still severely limited at low altitudes (according to one report, to Mach 0.8), but the 25M is said to have a low-level interception capability 'somewhat comparable to Flogger'. The only visible distinguishing feature of the 25M is an undernose sensor similar to the IR fairing carried by the 23MF. The new-generation MiG-31 Foxhound is described separately.

Compared with the MiG-25 interceptor, the reconnaissance versions have a wing of reduced area, with slightly less span and constant sweep from root to tip. The nose radar is removed, giving a conical nose offering reduced drag; inside this (in the basic version known to NATO as 'Foxbat-B) are five large vertical, forward oblique, lateral and panoramic cameras and a SLAR 'looking' through a dielectric panel on the left side of the nose. Doppler radar is believed to be fitted, as on many of the interceptor version. 'Foxbat-D' is a less common variant with a much larger SLAR installation and probably IR linescan but no cameras. About 160 MiG-25Rs of both models are estimated to be in Soviet service, plus about 45 with foreign customers, including eight with No 106 Sqn, Indian AF.

The MiG-25U trainer has the instructor cockpit in front of and below the original cockpit (occupied by the pupil), which is not only the reverse of normal procedure but means that the extra cockpit displaces the radar and other sensors (but not fuel).

Below: Showing one of the first MiG-25 interceptors, with pairs of IR and radar AA-6 missiles, this is still the best colour picture available. Today's MiG-25M has a nose similar to the MiG-23MF, with different radar and a forward-looking IR sensor.

MiG-27 (Flogger) and variants

Origin: The OKB named for Mikoyan/Guryevich, Soviet Union.
Type: Close-support and attack aircraft.
Engine: One 25,350lb (11,500kg) thrust Tumanskii R-29-300 augmented turbofan.
Dimensions: Span (72° sweep) 26ft 9⅔in (8.17m), (16°) 46ft 9in (14.25m); length 54ft (16.46m); height 14ft 9in (4.5m); wing area 293.4ft² (27.26m²).
Weights: (Estimated) Empty 24,800lb (11,250kg); loaded (clean) 35,000lb (15,876kg); max loaded 45,000lb (20,410kg).
Performance: Max speed (clean, hi altitude) 1,056mph (1,700km/h, Mach 1.6); (clean, lo) 722mph (1,162km/h, Mach 0.95); service ceiling 49,000ft (14,935m); combat radius (hi-lo-hi, 4,410lb/2,000kg external attack load) 311 miles (500km); ferry range (three tanks) 1,550 miles (2,500km).
Armament: One 23mm six-barrel rotary gun; up to 9,920lb (4,500kg) of external ordnance on eight pylons (two non-swivelling on outer wings, usable only for low-speed ferry tanks, two beneath gloves, two beneath inlet ducts and two on flanks of rear fuselage aft of landing gears); missiles include AS-7 and AS-14.
History: First flight 1968; service entry believed 1974.
Users: Afghanistan, Algeria, Bulgaria, Cuba, Czechoslovakia, East Germany, Egypt, Ethiopia, India, Iraq, Libya, Poland, Soviet Union, Sudan, Syria, Vietnam.

The MiG-27 is a dedicated subsonic low-level attack aircraft with a simplified propulsion system making no attempt to fly fast at high altitude. Compared with the MiG-23, it has a new nose with a downward-sloping, broad profile — resulting in the pilot nickname 'Ducknose' — not only giving a better forward view but also accommodating every desired avionics item for the surface attack mission, in place of a radar. Even the cockpit is repositioned at a higher level with a deeper hinged hood and windshield to give the pilot the best possible view ahead. A further change is the fitting of tyres of greater size and reduced inflation pressure for operations from rough, unpaved airstrips. The engine has a smaller afterburner with a simple nozzle matched to maximum thrust at take-off and in low-level missions; the nozzle is noticeably shorter than that of the MiG-23 family.

The oblique forward 'chisel' window covers a laser ranger and marked-target seeker. The small radome at the tip of the nose is for air-to-air ranging in conjunction with the gun. Under the nose is a doppler navigation radar, and further aft on each side are small blisters over CW target-illuminating radars. Aerials on the nose include the matched trio for IFF and the forward-pointing ILS, matched by a similar probe aerial on the fin facing aft. Sirena 3 radar homing and warning uses aerials on the leading edges and tail in the usual way, while forward-pointing pods on the fixed wing-glove leading edges are thought to be an ASM guidance transmitter (left) and an active ECM jammer transmitter (right).

Since 1980 the main production version has had a kinked taileron trailing edge, long leading-edge root extension strakes, a complete revision of the nose sensors with changes in external appearance, and no bullet avionics fairings on the wing gloves. Most MiG-27s have thick armour plates attached on the outside of the fuselage on each side of the cockpit.

Some of this family (the MiG-23BN series, 'Flogger-F' and -H) have the propulsion system of the MiG-23 fighter. This mixed model has been exported to many countries, including India, but the version licence-built by HAL is the MiG-27M 'Flogger-J', a pure attack variant with the root strakes. The R-60 dogfight AAM is also licensed to HAL.

Above: A Soviet-built MiG-23BN of the Indian Air Force, 80 of which were delivered.

Left: This MiG-23BN ('Flogger-H') serves with the Czech Air Force. This version has body pylons inboard, not under the inlet ducts, a variable-geometry propulsion system with vertical-sided inlets, and main tyres similar to the interceptor (thus, narrower than those of the MiG-27, which require bulged sides to the fuselage around the main-gear bays).

MiG-29 (Fulcrum)

Origin: The OKB named for Mikoyan/Guryevich, Soviet Union.
Type: Multirole fighter and attack aircraft.
Engines: Two Tumanskii R-33D augmented turbofans, each rated at 11,243lb (5,100kg) dry and 18,300lb (8,300kg) with max augmentation.
Dimensions: Span 34ft 5½ in (10.5m); length (inc probe) 56ft 5¼ in (17.2m); height 17ft 2¾ in (5.25m); wing area 358ft² (33.3m²).
Weights: Empty 17,250lb (7,825kg); loaded (fighter mission) 36,375lb (16,500kg); max about 39,680lb (18,000kg).
Performance: (Estimated) Max speed (hi altitude) 1,525mph (2,455km/h, Mach 2.3), (sea level) 910mph (1,470km/h, Mach 1.2); sustained turn rate (15,000ft/4,572m, Mach 0.9) 16°/sec (instantaneous rate 21°/sec, pulling 9g); max climb rate 50,000ft (15,240m)/min; service ceiling 58,000ft (17,680m); combat radius (hi) 715 miles (1,150km).
Armament: One six-barrel 30mm gun in left wing root; three pylons under each wing for six AA-10 medium-range radar-guided AAMs or six close-range AA-11 AAMs, or for wide range of attack stores including bombs, rockets, missiles and cluster dispensers.
History: First flight not later than April 1979; service entry October 1983.
Users: Soviet Union; soon to include India, Syria and other countries.

On 1 July 1986 six unarmed but otherwise combat-ready MiG-29 fighters of the VVS (Soviet Air Force) arrived over the Finnish air base at Kuopio-Rissala. After putting on a brief display they landed to begin a goodwill (and perhaps sales-promotion) visit. Previously these fighters, dubbed 'Fulcrum' by NATO, had been known only from small satellite images from overhead (and, in 1986, by a series of good take-off pictures).

From the start it was evident the MiG-29 was utterly unlike any previous MiG, and much more like the American F-14, F-15 and F-18. Aerodynamically it very closely resembles the bigger Su-27, showing that tradition is being maintained and a TsAGI (Central Aero and Hydrodynamics Institute) 'best configuration' has been built by the two OKBs but in different sizes. The one way in which the Soviet fighters differ from the US types is that they have a low-mounted wing, though this is obscured by the fact that the giant engines are then added beneath the wing to give a rear half looking like an F-15. The engine installations and main landing gears strongly resemble those of the F-14, but a unique feature is that the giant oblique inlets are automatically shut off by hinged doors, probably triggered by pressure on the nosewheel leg. The engines then 'breathe' through a huge aperture in the top of the wing apex section, normally closed by five hinged doors. This eliminates ingestion of foreign objects, slush and other material.

There is large internal fuel capacity between the engines, in the wings and rear fuselage. Structurally, the outward-canted vertical tails are mounted on the outer sides of the 'rear fuselage', which is actually the engine bay below

Below: This MiG-29 visiting Finland has automatically closed the doors to its main engine inlets, opening the row of alternative inlet apertures above the wing, preventing foreign-object damage.

Above: This view shows the simple, bold geometry of this very important fighter, with giant engine installations entirely under the wing and its huge forward apex extension.

wing level, the fuselage proper having (as in the F-14) tapered off to nothing. No longer does the tail have to be detachable; the engines can be withdrawn direct to the rear, as in some previous MiG twins. As noted, the main gears retract as in the F-14, folding forwards with the wheels turning through 90° to lie flat inside the wing root above the leg. The twin-wheel steerable nose gear, which has to be very large, retracts backwards into a bay between the inlet ducts.

The swept wings have full-span leading-edge flaps except over the curved streamwise tips, and on the trailing edge are plain flaps and outboard ailerons, only about 25° of flap being used for landing. Computers schedule the wing camber for maximum manoeuvrability, with the primary roll control at high speeds being the slab tailerons which extend far aft of the engine nozzles. The one-piece rudders are quite small. Each wing is attached to a giant blended inboard portion which provides considerable internal volume and also extends forwards in an apex section to provide a large flat undersurface above the inlets. Most of the apex leading edge is occupied by RWRs, ESM aerials and other avionics. In the nose is the advanced pulse-doppler radar (which, the US insists, was developed with the aid of documents secretly obtained on the APG-65 radar of the F-18). There are the usual comprehensive fits of IFF, ILS and communications, as well as a remarkably large IR sensor under a transparent dome offset to the right in front of the windshield.

Airbrakes are mounted above the rear fuselage (and possibly between the jetpipes). In the tail is the box for the cruciform braking parachute. A notable feature of this shape of aircraft (and thus of the Su-27 also) is the great height of the fuselage off the ground, which means that ladders and trestles are needed for access to many of the LRUs (line replaceable units) and other items. The payoff is the superb engine installation, which plays a big part in making this one of the best air-combat fighters yet created. Almost the only real criticism must be the way Soviet designers continue to impede the pilot's view with devices both inside and outside the cockpit.

By late 1986 about 300 MiG-29s were probably in combat units; the official Western assessment of 'more than 150' seems over-cautious. India selected the type two years previously, but deferred the first batch of 40 to obtain a newer version, and expects Hindustan Aeronautics to build it under licence. Another early customer was Syria, which was expecting the first batch of a total of 80 aircraft as this book was being written in autumn 1986. Jordan has also been offered the MiG-29, in February 1986, and is likely to become a customer.

MiG-31 (Foxhound)

Origin: The OKB named for Mikoyan/Guryevich, Soviet Union.
Type: Long-range interceptor.
Engines: Two 30,865lb (14,000kg) thrust R-31F afterburning turbojets.
Dimensions: (Estimated) Span 45ft 10½in (14m); length 70ft 6½in (21.5m); height 18ft 6in (5.63m); wing area 602ft² (56m²).
Weights: (Estimated) Empty 48,115lb (21,825kg); max 90,725lb (41,050kg).
Performance: (Estimated) Max speed (hi, 8 AAM) 1,586mph (2,553km/h, Mach 2.4), (sea level) 900mph (1,450km/h, Mach 1.18); service ceiling 75,500ft (23,000m); combat radius (hi, intercept) 1,305 miles (2,100km).
Armament: Eight AA-9 AAMs, or four AA-9 and four R-23R or R60s.
History: First flight probably about 1977; service delivery not later than 1981.
User: Soviet Union.

Below: This drawing shows the longer afterburners and wing-root extensions of the MiG-31.

Though based closely on the MiG-25, the MiG-31 is a completely new aircraft. Structurally the airframe has been restressed for manoeuvrability at all altitudes. The MiG-31 can outrun almost anything else in the sky, and has a complete capability against multiple targets at all heights, including ground-hugging lo attack.

Among the major differences compared with the MiG-25 are the addition of a second crew member, the elimination of the wing-tip anti-flutter bodies and the ability to carry eight missiles. The AAMs are smaller than the AA-6 but have a similar punch and require no inflight guidance. MiG-31s have demonstrated very great radar range and TWS capability while intercepting RPV targets including simulated cruise missiles at Vladimirovka, a test range on the Caspian. Another report specifically states that radar-guided missiles fired from high-flying MiG-31s have intercepted targets flying at about 200ft (90m).

There are two wing pylons, and four on the flanks of the fuselage. Even the AA-9 is still a substantial missile, considerably bigger than Sparrow, and eight would impose a serious drag penalty. Precisely how all eight are carried has not yet been published. Early reports of the MiG-31 invariably referred to an internal gun, but this is not mentioned in any of the nine Pentagon-based reports published since November 1983. What is emphasized, however, is that four regiments of MiG-31s (about 150 aircraft) were already operational with Voyska PVO forces by late 1986, with output from a factory at Gorkii building up all the time.

In 1986 it was announced by the US Department of Defense that there is also a reconnaissance version, which one may assume to be the MiG-31R. Roughly one-quarter of the output is of this version, though the basic interceptor remains the MiG-31 with four AA-9 missiles carried in pairs under the fuselage and pairs of smaller R-60R or R-23R/T missiles carried on two wing pylons.

Below: This MiG-31, based on the Kola Peninsula in the Soviet Arctic, shows the fuselage carriage of four giant AA-9 missiles, each very similar to the American Phoenix. Four more might be carried under the wings, all with long-range 'look-down' capability.

Mitsubishi F-1, T-2

Origin: Mitsubishi Heavy Industries Ltd, Japan.
Type: (T-2) Two-seat supersonic trainer; (T-2A) armed trainer; (F-1) single-seat close-support fighter-bomber.
Engines: Two Ishikawajima-Harima TF40-801A (licence-built Rolls-Royce/Turboméca Adour 102) augmented turbofans with max rating of 7,140lb (3,238kg).
Dimensions: Span 25ft 10in (7.87m); length 58ft 7in (17.86m); height (T-2) 14ft 7in (4.44m), (F-1) 14ft 9in (4.49m); wing area 227.9ft² (21.7m²).
Weights: Empty (T-2) 13,905lb (6,307kg), 14,330lb (6,500kg); loaded (T-2, clean) 21,274lb (9,650kg), (T-2, max) 28,440lb (12,900kg); (F-1, max) 30,200lb (13,700kg).
Performance: Max speed (clean, gross weight) 1,056mph (1,700km/h, Mach 1.6); initial climb rate 19,680ft (6,000m)/min; service ceiling 50,025ft (15,250m); take-off run (F-1, max weight) 4,200ft (1,280m); range (T-2 with external tanks) 1,610 miles (2,593km), (F-1 with eight 500lb bombs) 700 miles (1,126km).
Armament: (T-2A, F-1) One 20mm JM-61 multibarrel gun under left side of cockpit floor; pylon hardpoints under centreline and inboard and outboard on wings, with light stores attachments at tips. Total weapon load (T-2A) normally 2,000lb (907kg), (F-1) 6,000lb (2,722kg) comprising 12 500lb bombs, eight 500lb plus two tanks of 183gal (832l), or two 1,300lb (590kg) ASM-1 anti-ship missiles, and four Sidewinders, or three 183gal drop tanks.
History: First flight (XT-2) 20 July 1971, (T-2A) January 1975, (FST-2) June 1975; service delivery (T-2A) March 1975, (F-1) 1977.
User: Japan.

The T-2 trainer was strongly influenced by the Anglo-French Jaguar and has the same configuration and engines. Unusual in being supersonic, it has a simple Mitsubishi Electric search/ranging radar and a Thomson-CSF HUD. The

Below: The first production F-1, which first flew on 16 June 1977. Airframe, engines and aircraft systems are almost identical to those of the T-2 trainer, though the rear cockpit is an avionics bay.

JASDF bought a total of 28 trainers, plus 58 of the armed T-2A combat trainer version. All were delivered by 1984, one being grossly modified to serve as a CCV research aircraft.

The F-1, originally known as the FST-2, has the same airframe, engines and systems, but is a single seater, the rear cockpit being occupied by avionics and having an opaque metal canopy. A Ferranti inertial nav/attack system is fitted, together with a different Mitsubishi radar with air-to-air and air-to-ground modes, a weapon-aiming computer, a radar altimeter and RHAWS (radar homing and warning system), the weapon system being modified from 1982 to handle the locally developed ASM-1 anti-ship missile.

Total procurement of the F-1 was 77, all of which will probably have been delivered by the time this book appears. They serve with the 3rd Squadron of the 3rd Air Wing at Misawa and with the complete 8th Air Wing at Tsuiki. The JASDF had planned to order a replacement (FS-X), but the daunting development cost has led to a decision to carry out a life-extension programme on the F-1 to keep it operational until at least 1993.

Above: This T-2 was converted into a CCV (control-configured vehicle) research aircraft. It has three canard controls, manoeuvring flaps on the wings and triplex digital fly-by-wire controls.

Nanchang Q-5 (Fantan)

Origin: Chinese national factory at Nanchang, design based on J-6 (MiG-19).

Type: Close-support attack fighter.

Engines: Two Shenyang WP-6 afterburning turbojets (derived from Soviet Tumanskii R-9BF-811), each rated at 7,165lb (3,250kg) thrust.

Dimensions: Span 31ft 10in (9.7m); length (inc probe) 54ft 10½ in (16.73m); height 14ft 9½ in (4.51m); wing area 300.85ft² (27.95m²).

Weights: Empty 14,317lb (6,494kg); loaded (clean) 21,010lb (9,530kg), (max external stores) 26,455lb (12,000kg).

Performance: Max speed (hi, clean) 740mph (1,190km/h, Mach 1.12), (sea level, clean) 752mph (1,210km/h, Mach 0.99); service ceiling 52,500ft (16,000m); take-off run (max weight) 4,100ft (1,250m); combat radius (max bombs, no afterburner, hi-lo-hi) 373 miles (600km), (lo-lo-lo) 248 miles (400km).

Armament: Two Type 23-2 23mm single-barrel guns, each with 100 rounds, in wing roots; internal bomb bay usually occupied by fuel tank, leaving four fuselage pylons each rated at 551lb (250kg) and four wing pylons, those inboard of landing gear being rated at 551lb (250kg) and those outboard being plumbed for 167gal (760l) drop tanks. Max bomb or other stores load usually 4,410lb (2,000kg).

History: First flight 1972; service delivery believed 1976.

Users: China, North Korea, Pakistan.

Below: An early, unpainted Q-5 in the PLA Air Force. Under the nose are the ADF, radio altimeter and landing light, while on the starboard side is a ram-air cooling inlet absent from the A-5 and later models.

Above: Q-5s on the production line at Nanchang. Manufacture is continuing, and in 1986 a major contract was signed with Aeritalia under which the Italian company will supply upgraded avionics for a new export version designated A-5M. Equipment will include a digital navigation keyboard and a HUD (head-up display), plus other items similar to those on the Italian version of the AMX.

The first major military aircraft to be designed in the People's Republic, the Q-5 was based on the J-6 but differs in almost every part. The chief change was to extend the forward fuselage, terminate the air inlet ducts in lateral inlets and add an internal weapons bay (which today is almost always occupied by fuel). The wings were extended at the roots, which also increased the track of the landing gear (which is strengthened to handle the greater weights), and the vertical tail was made taller. The underwing spoilers were omitted, and the Gouge flaps modified. The cockpit was redesigned, and enclosed by an upward-hinged canopy leading into a different fuselage spine. There were many systems changes, the most important being an increase in internal fuel capacity of nearly 70 per cent. Flight Refuelling Ltd have designed a receiver probe installation, compatible with H-6 (Tu-16 'Badger') tankers.

Performance proved adequate with the original engines, though at high weights a good runway is needed, and a braking parachute is normally streamed (later aircraft have it housed in a pod below the rudder as in later J-6s).

At first it was thought the reason for using lateral inlets was to enable a radar to be installed, but this was mistaken. Q-5 development aircraft have flown with radar, and a small gunsight ranging set is fitted to some recent machines, but no variant has gone into production with a major radar. Avionics are described as fully adequate for visual attack missions, including the 'High Fix' gun-ranging radar.

The Pakistan AF, the first customer for the A-5 export version, is delighted with the initial batch of 42 received in 1983 and equipping Nos 16, 26 and 7 Sqns. Eventually the PAF expects to receive 140 A-5s, to arm eight squadrons and an OCU.

The photographs so far seen of the A-5 show it to be cleaner than regular Q-5s, though the avionic standards are said to be similar. Chinese Q-5s can carry nuclear bombs of from 5 to 20kT yield, and the usual method of delivery of these is a toss. Conventional weapons are usually aimed by the SH-1J optical sight in a dive attack.

Northrop F-5

Origin: Northrop Corporation, USA; licence manufacture by KAL (South Korea), FFA (Switzerland), AIDC (Taiwan) and possibly TUSAS (Turkey); early models by Canada, the Netherlands and Spain.

Type: Light tactical fighter and attack/reconnaissance aircraft.

Engines: Two General Electric J85 afterburning turbojets, (A,B) 4,080lb (1,850kg) thrust J85-13 or -13A, (E,F) 5,000lb (2,270kg) thrust -21A.

Dimensions: Span (A,B) 25ft 3in (7.7m), (A,B over tip tanks) 25ft 10in (7.87m), (E,F) 26ft 8in (8.13m), (E,F over AAMs) 27ft 11in (8.53m); length (A) 47ft 2in (14.38m), (B) 46ft 4in (14.12m), (E) 48ft 2in (14.68m), (F) 51ft 7in (15.72m); height overall (E) 13ft 7in (4.06m); wing area (A,B) 170ft² (15.79m²), (E,F) 186ft² (17.3m²).

Weights: Empty (A) 8,085lb (3,667kg), (B) 8,361lb (3,792kg), (E) 9,683lb (4,392kg), (F) 10,567lb (4,793kg); max loaded (A) 20,576lb (9,333kg), (B) 20,116lb (9,124kg), (E) 24,722lb (11,214kg), (F) 25,225lb (11,442kg).

Performance: Max speed at 36,000ft (11,000m) (A) 925mph (1,489km/h, Mach 1.4), (B) 886mph (1,425km/h, Mach 1.34), (E) 1,077mph (1,734km/h, Mach 1.63), (F) 1,011mph (1,628km/h, Mach 1.53); typical cruising speed 562mph (904km/h, Mach 0.85); initial climb rate (A,B) 28,700ft (8,750m)/min, (E) 34,500ft (10,516m)/min, (F) 32,890ft (10,250m)/min; service ceiling (all) about 51,000ft (15,540m); combat radius with max weapon load and allowances (A, hi-lo-hi) 215 miles (346km), (E, lo-lo-lo) 138 miles (222km); range with max fuel (hi, tanks dropped, with reserves) (A) 1,565 miles (2,518km), (E) 1,779 miles (2,863km).

Armament: (A,B) Military load 6,200lb (2,812kg) including two 20mm M-39 guns each with 280 rounds, and wide variety of underwing stores, plus AIM-9 AAMs for air combat; (E,F) wide range of ordnance to total of 7,000lb (3,175kg) not including two (F-5F, one) M-39A2 guns each with 280 rounds and two AIM-9 missiles on tip rails.

History: First flight (N-156C) 30 July 1959, (production F-5A) October 1963, (F-5E) 11 August 1972.

Users: Bahrain, Brazil, Canada, Chile, Ethiopia, Greece, Honduras, Indonesia, Iran, Jordan, Kenya, South Korea, Libya, Malaysia, Mexico, Morocco, Netherlands, Norway, Philippines, Saudi Arabia, Singapore, Spain, Sudan, Switzerland, Taiwan, Thailand, Tunisia, Turkey, USA (AF, Navy), Venezuela, Vietnam, Yemen Arab Rep.

Cheap, simple, delightful to handle and supersonic, the small twin-jets from Northrop have found a ready market all over the world. The F-5A Freedom Fighter and F-5B tandem dual two-seater were followed by the F-5E Tiger II. This has a wider fuselage increasing internal fuel to 563.7gal (2,563l), leading-edge root extensions, uprated engines, an extensible nose leg, manoeuvre flaps, a gyro sight, an arrester hook and an Emerson radar with a fair capability against air or ship targets at ranges to 23 miles (37km).

Individual customers have asked for extras, Saudi Arabian aircraft having a more comprehensive avionics fit including a Litton INS, comprehensive RWR and chaff/flare dispensers and Maverick ASMs. Switzerland specified anti-skid brakes and a different ECM fit. Improvements that became standard during production included auto manoeuvre flaps on both leading and trailing edges, a flattened 'shark nose' and larger leading-edge extensions.

The F-5F two-seater retains one gun and external weapons. The RF-5E Tigereye replaces the radar by a new, longer nose with a different profile in which can be installed a forward oblique KS-87D1 frame camera and any of a growing series of pallets on which are mounted selected sensors.

By 1986 Northrop and its licensees had delivered over 1,300 F-5Es and -Fs, with production continuing at a reduced rate.

Below: The F-5E is used by the USAF not in an operational but in a training role, honing fighter-pilot skills with four Aggressor squadrons. Two such units are at Nellis AFB, whose aircraft are seen here; one is at RAF Alconbury and the fourth in the Philippines.

Panavia Tornado ADV

Origin: Panavia Aircraft GmbH, an international company formed by British Aerospace, MBB and Aeritalia.
Type: Long-range, all-weather interceptor.
Engines: Two Turbo-Union RB199 Mk 104 augmented turbofans, each rated at 18,100lb (8,212kg) thrust with full afterburner.
Dimensions: Span (25°) 45ft 7¼in (13.9m), (67°) 28ft 2½ft (8.6m); length 59ft 4in (18.08m); height 18ft 8½in (5.7m); wing area not published.
Weights: Empty (equipped) 31,970lb (14,500kg); take-off (clean, max internal fuel) 47,500lb (21,546kg); max 61,700lb (27,986kg).
Performance: Max speed (clean, hi) about 1,500mph (2,414km/h, Mach 2.27); intercept radius (subsonic mission) over 1,151 miles (1,853km); combat mission (max AAM load), 2hr 20min on station at distance of 375 miles (602km) from base with allowance for combat.
Armament: One 27mm Mauser cannon, four Sky Flash (later Amraam) recessed under fuselage and two AIM-9L Sidewinder AAMs (later Asraam).
History: First flight 27 October 1979; service delivery late 1984; operational late 1985.
Users: Oman, Saudi Arabia, UK (RAF).

Though it is a purely British development, the ADV (air-defence variant) of Tornado is produced by the same tri-national airframe and engine groupings as is the IDS series, and in due course it is likely to become the most widely used model, with greater export interest from more countries. It is unquestionably the most efficient long-range interceptor in the world, outperforming all known rivals in almost all respects, with engines of amazingly small size and low fuel burn. ▶

Below: No 229 Operational Conversion Unit had about 20 aircraft as this book was written, variously Mks 2, 2A and (ZE154 onwards) 3. A proportion at this unit are dual-control (Type AT) trainers.

Above: Banking away, this early Tornado F.2 shows its Sky Flash missiles recessed into the underside of the fuselage, which was made longer than that of the IDS version in order to accommodate them.

▶ Designated Tornado F.3 by the RAF, the interceptor has about 80 per cent commonality with the original IDS aircraft, and most of the airframe and aircraft systems are unchanged. The forward fuselage, made by BAe in any case, is completely new. This features a new pair of cockpits, with later electronic displays, different symbology, a greater processing and storage capacity and a wet-film HDD recorder; Marconi/Ferranti AI.24 Foxhunter FMICW radar, with a multimode lookup/lookdown TWS and missile guidance capability; the deletion of one of the two guns; the installation of a permanent FR probe fully retractable on the left side; the installation of a ram-air turbine giving full hydraulic system power at high altitudes with main engines inoperative, down to below 230mph (370km/h); and the addition of the Cossor 3500 series IFF, Singer ECM-resistant data link (with an AWACS, for example, or ground stations), and a second INS.

Other airframe changes include the forward extension of the fixed wing gloves, giving a major change in lift and agility, the provision of 200gal (909l) of extra fuel in the extended fuselage, and belly recesses for four Sky Flash (later AIM-120A) medium-range missiles, with twin-ram, cartridge-powered ejection giving clean launch at maximum negative g. The engines have various upratings which at high speeds and altitudes become large and significant, with extended jetpipes which improve afterbody shape and reduce drag; they also have digital control. The only item not mentioned in connection with the production F.3 is the magnifying optical VAS (visual augmentation system) for the positive identification of aircraft at great distances, which was regarded as a crucial item early in the programme.

By mid-1984 British Aerospace had almost completed the basic flight development programme with the three F.2 prototypes, and had delivered the first two F.2 production aircraft. The latter are both ATs (dual pilot ADV trainers), which after a spell at Boscombe Down cleared fully operational F.2s to form the OCU (Operational Conversion Unit) at Coningsby in September 1984.

The first production batch of 15 aircraft was complete by this time, temporarily fitted with Mk 103 engines. The second and third RAF batches, numbering 52 and 92 aircraft and designated F.3, have the Mk 104 from the outset, as well as automatic schedule of wing-sweep and manoeuvre-devices (wing slats and flaps at 25° to 45° sweep) to give enhanced manoeuvrability with minimal pilot workload.

Above: Formating on a photographic C-130, this F.2 can probably fly more slowly under full control than any other fighter in the world.

Above: Looking down on an early F.2 at maximum sweep. The first RAF squadron to convert is No 29, based like 229 OCU at Coningsby.

Updates planned for the future include still more powerful engines, even larger (495gal/2,250l) drop tanks, the AIM-120A (Amraam) and Asraam missiles and further improvements to the avionics. All round performance has been demonstrated as equal to or better than prediction, with acceleration remaining 'healthy' at Mach 2, and 800kt (912mph/1,483km/h) indicated airspeed being registered at medium altitudes (true speed being much greater) and at heights down to 2,000ft (610m). Few if any other fighters can match this.

From early 1986 the Tornado F.3 began to take its place in the RAF, protecting the UK Air Defence Region. It will equip seven squadrons. The first export order was eight for the Sultan of Oman's Air Force; later the same year (1985) a contract for 24 was signed by Saudi Arabia. With 165 for the RAF, this makes a total of 197.

Panavia Tornado IDS

Origin: Panavia Aircraft GmbH, an international company formed by British Aerospace, MBB and Aeritalia.
Type: Two-seat multirole combat aircraft optimised for strike; (T) dual trainer.
Engines: Two Turbo-Union RB199 Mk 103 augmented turbofans each rated at 16,920lb (7,675kg) thrust with full afterburner.
Dimensions: Span (25°) 45ft 7¼in (13.9m), (67°) 28ft 2½in (8.6m); length 54ft 9½in (16.7m); height 18ft 8½in (5.7m); wing area not published.
Weights: Empty (equipped) 31,065lb (14,091kg); loaded (clean) about 45,000lb (20,411kg); max loaded about 60,000lb (18,150kg).
Performance: Max speed (clean, sea level) over 920mph (1,480km/h, Mach 1.2), (hi) over 1,450mph (2,335km/h, Mach 2.2); service ceiling over 50,000ft (15,240m); combat radius (8,000lb/3,629kg bombs, hi-lo-hi) 863 miles (1,390km).
Armament: Two 27mm Mauser cannon in lower forward fuselage; seven pylons, three tandem on body and four on the swing wings, for external load of up to 18,000lb (8,165kg).
History: First flight (prototype) 14 August 1974, (production IDS) July 1979; service delivery (IDS to trials unit) February 1978, (squadron service, RAF, Luftwaffe, Marineflieger) 1982.
Users: West Germany (Luftwaffe, Marineflieger), Italy, Saudi Arabia, UK (RAF).

The most important military aircraft in Western Europe, the Tornado was the outcome of the first multinational collaborative programme to embrace design and development as well as manufacture, and to lead to a completely successful exercise in both management and hardware.

Though from the start a multirole aircraft, the Tornado IDS (interdiction strike) is optimized for the long-range, all-weather, blind, first-pass attack mission against the most heavily defended surface targets, including ships. It is by far the most capable aircraft of its size ever built ▶

Above: Two GR.1s from RAF No 9 Sqn, on a training sortie from
Honington, pull up from terrain-hugging flight to reduce noise past a
Scottish town. Each has four 1,000lb bombs, two tanks and two Sky
Shadow ECM jammer pods. Much heavier loads can be carried.

Below: The chin-mounted laser stands out prominently under this IDS
aircraft for the Royal Saudi Air Force, on test before delivery in
February 1986. Saudi Arabia's 72 Tornados include 48 of this model.

► Features include a Texas Instruments multimode forward-looking radar with the option of various types of programmable software, a TFR (terrain-following radar), electrically signalled FBW (fly-by-wire) flight controls with artificial stability, fully variable supersonic inlets, advanced avionics systems to manage the array of stores which can be carried, and modern tandem cockpits with head-up and head-down displays in the front and three electronic displays in the back.

Among the stores which have been cleared are all tactical bombs of the four initial customers, nine rocket pods, Sidewinder AAMs, and Sea Eagle, Kormoran, Maverick, BLU-1B, GBU-15, Paveway, AS.30 and AS.30L, Martel (seldom to be carried), Aspide, Harm, Alarm, BL.755, JP.233 and MW-1; Harpoon and possibly other cruise missiles may be carried later.

Above: The Kormoran anti-ship missile is carried by Tornados of the German Marineflieger and also Italy's AMI, the latter's aircraft including this machine from the 156° Gruppo of the 36° Stormo, based at Gioia del Colle, in the 'heel' of the country.

Right: The main strength of the Luftwaffe's 212 IDS Tornados will lie in five fighter/bomber wings, JaBoG 31 to 34 and 38. This aircraft, painted in the latest camouflage scheme of grey and two shades of green, is assigned to JaBoG 38, at Jever.

All aircraft have two guns, Martin-Baker Mk 10 automatic zero/zero seats, a gas-turbine APU which is self-cooling and can be left running on the ground, automatically scheduled lift-dumpers, pre-armed engine reversers, anti-skid brakes and (as a further option) a braking parachute. There is provision, so far exercised only by the RAF, to bolt on an FR probe package above the right side below the canopy. All sub-types have very comprehensive EW systems, with advanced RHAWS and either the Elettronica EL/73 deception jammer and ELT 553 ECM pod, or the Marconi Avionics Sky Shadow.

The ECR (electronic combat and reconnaissance) variant is an extremely advanced derivative first bought by the Luftwaffe. Its digital data bus ties a FLIR, ELS (emitter locator system), I²S (infra-red imaging system) and extremely complete processing, storage and display systems.

Deliveries began in 1980 to the TTTE (Tornado Trinational Training Establishment), located at RAF Cottesmore in England. This has a strength of 50 aircraft, a high proportion being dual-pilot trainers for pilot conversion, the rest being for training navigators and complete crews. Aircraft from all three nations are used, the crews likewise being completely multinational until they actually pair up for final training as a team. By 1982 two further major training units were operational, that for the Luftwaffe (WaKo) being at Erding and for the RAF (TWCU) at Honington.

RAF squadrons began with Nos 9, 27 and 617 in England, followed by eight in RAF Germany, 15 and 16 (ex-Buccaneer) at Laarbruch, all four squadrons in the former Jaguar wing at Brüggen, No 9 (from Honington) and, in 1986, equipment of No 2 Sqn with aircraft specially configured for reconnaissance.

Marineflieger MFG 1 and 2 are both converted from the F-104G, while the Luftwaffe is converting five JaboG wings, Nos 31 to 34 and No 38. Italy's AMI is using 54 aircraft to replace the F/RF-104G in the 154°, 155° and 156° Gruppi, with further dual-pilot aircraft equipping the 3° GEV (maintenance/training squadron) at Cameri.

Total national commitments, all delivered or in process of manufacture as this was written, are as follows: RAF, 219 with designation GR.1 (plus a pre-production machine brought up to GR.1 standard); Marineflieger, 112; Luftwaffe, 212 plus 35 of the ECR version; and AMI, 99 plus one pre-production aircraft updated. This gives a total of 699 (929 including ADV versions), of which 580 had been delivered by year-end 1986. Saudi Arabia is to receive 72, of which the first six were delivered in summer 1986.

Saab 37 (AJ, SF, SH, SK) Viggen

Origin: Saab-Scania AB, Sweden.
Type: (AJ) Single-seat all-weather attack aircraft; (SF) armed photo-reconnaissance aircraft; (SH) armed sea surveillance aircraft; (SK) dual trainer.
Engine: One Svenska Flygmotor RM8A (licence-built Pratt & Whitney JT8D turbofan redesigned in Sweden for Mach 2 with afterburner) rated at 25,970lb (11,790kg) thrust will full afterburner.
Dimensions: Span 34ft 9⅓in (10.6m); length (AJ) 53ft 5¾in (16.3m); height (most) 18ft 4½in (5.6m), (SK) 19ft 4½in (5.9m); wing area 495.1ft² (46m²).
Weights: Empty (all) about 27,000lb (12,250kg); loaded (AJ, normal armament) 35,275lb (16,000kg), (AJ, max weapons) 45,195lb (20,500kg).
Performance: Max speed (clean) about 1,320mph (2,135km/h, Mach 2), or Mach 1.1 at sea level; initial climb rate about 40,000ft (12,200m)/min (time from start of take-off run to 32,800ft/10,000m = 100sec); service ceiling over 60,000ft (18,300m); tactical radius (external stores, no drop tanks, hi-lo-hi) over 620 miles (1,000km).
Armament: Seven pylons (optionally nine) for aggregate external load of 13,200lb (6,000kg), including RB04, 05 or 75 missiles for attack, and RB24 and 28 missiles for defence.
History: First flight 8 February 1967, (production AJ) 23 February 1971; service delivery (AJ) June 1971.
User: Sweden (RSAF).

Like all Swedish programmes for combat aircraft, the Type 37 Viggen (Thunderbolt) has been wholly successful, producing five sub-types of the same basic machine, each tailored to a different primary role, within budget and on time. The first and still most numerous version is the AJ37, dedicated mainly to attack on surface targets and ships.

The design was biased in favour of STOL operations from stretches of country highways and dirt tracks. The big afterburning engine gives high thrust for a quick getaway, though at the cost of fuel consumption. The large delta wing and canard foreplanes form a powerful high-lift combination, and can also be used to pull tight turns in close combat. On landing the Viggen can be brought in at only 137mph (220km/h), slammed on to the ground in a

Below: Standard equipment for most AJ37s is a centreline tank, a SATT AQ31 ECM jammer and a Philips BOZ 9 dispenser pod.

Above: Reconnaissance versions include the specialized maritime SH37 and the overland SF37 illustrated. The SF has cameras in place of radar, as well as IR linescan, elint receivers and recorders, and (visible here) a Red Baron multisensor pod for night reconnaissance.

carrier-type, no-flare impact, and at once given full reverse thrust and maximum no-skid wheel braking.

The AJ37 equips two squadrons of F6 Wing at Karlsborg, two squadrons of F7 at Satenäs and one squadron of F15 at Söderhamm. Variants of the AJ37 are the SF37 and SH37 reconnaissance models.

The SH37, for maritime use, replaced the S32C Lansen in F13 Wing and in mixed SH/SF Wings F17 and F21. It is used primarily to survey, register and report all maritime activity near Sweden. It has the basic airframe of the AJ37, with an LM Ericsson multimode radar, a Marconi HUD and a central digital computer, with an added camera for recording the radar displays. The three fuselage pylons carry a large tank on the centreline, a night reconnaissance pod with IR linescan and LLTV on the left and a Red Baron or long-range camera pod on the right. Inboard wing pylons can carry active or passive ECM jammer pods, and very complete elint and EW recorders are carried, together with a tape recorder and a data camera.

The SF37, which serves with the same three wings as the SH, has no main radar, and its slim, pointed nose houses four vertical or oblique cameras for low-level use, two long-range vertical high-altitude cameras and VKA IR linescan. Also installed in the fuselage are the camera sight, an IR sensor and EW systems including and RWR and elint recorders. The SK37 is a dual trainer with a raised rear cockpit and a taller fin with a sweptback tip. The JA37 interceptor is described separately.

Below: The AJ37 can get away very quickly in full afterburner, though at the cost of high fuel consumption. Note the neat main gears.

Saab JA37 Viggen

Origin: Saab-Scania AB, Sweden.
Type: All-weather interceptor with attack capability.
Engine: One Volvo Flygmotor RM8B augmented turbofan rated at 16,203lb (7,350kg) dry and 28,108lb (12,750kg) with max augmentation.
Dimensions: Span 34ft 9⅓in (10.6m); length 53ft 9¾in (16.4m); height 19ft 4⅓in (5.9m); wing area 495.1ft² (46m²), foreplanes 66.74ft² (6.2m²).
Weights: Empty, not published; loaded (clean) about 33,070lb (15,000kg); 'with normal armament' about 37,478lb (17,000kg).
Performance: Max speed with AAMs (hi altitude) over 1,320mph (2,135km/h, Mach 2), (sea level) 910mph (1,470km/h Mach 1.2); take-off/landing runs, about 1,500ft (457m); time to 32,800ft (10,000m) from brakes-release, less than 1min 40sec; tactical radius (external armament, hi-lo-hi) over 620 miles (1,000km), (lo-lo-lo) over 311 miles (500km).
Armament: One 30mm Oerlikon KCA cannon with 150 rounds; three body pylons and four underwing, for normal interception armament of two RB71 (BAe Sky Flash) and four RB24 (AIM-9 Sidewinder) AAMs; attack loads can include four launchers each housing six 135mm heavy rockets.
History: First flight (modified AJ development aircraft) 1974, (production JA) 4 November 1977; squadron delivery 1979.
User: Sweden.

The final version of the Viggen, and the only one now in production, the JA37 fighter is a much more extensive redesign than all previous variants, and its development cost more than the entire design and development of the original AJ model. Its performance is optimized for interception at a distance, using radar-guided medium-range Sky Flash AAMs (for which the Swedish Air Force has placed a large follow-on order), and for close combat at all altitudes.

The engine has a different match of fans and compressors, and gives higher thrust.

The airframe has underwing fairings for four elevon power units on each wing instead of three, and the vertical tail (which folds flat for entry into low-ceiling underground hangars) is the same taller, swept-tip type as that on the SK37 dual trainer version.

Though no longer new in concept, the avionics of the JA37 stand comparison with those of the F-15 or any other fighter in service today. The main radar is an Ericsson UAP-1023 pulse-doppler set operating in I/J-band and giving outstanding look-down performance against low-flying small targets in adverse environments and in the presence of intense ECM (the same can, of course, be said of the BAe Dynamics Sky Flash missile, used as the RB71). Other equipment includes an advanced Marconi Avionics HUD, a Singer-Kearfott main digital computer, a Garrett digital air-data computer, an advanced ILS, and outstandingly comprehensive EW systems (which make those of many NATO aircraft look pathetic). The single gun, under the fuselage, is more powerful than any other 30mm gun in a Western fighter (except for the unique weapon used in the anti-tank A-10A).

The JA37 normally flies with a large centreline drop tank, and it can carry various surface-attack weapons if necessary. Current production machines are painted air-superiority grey, which is being retroactively applied to aircraft in service. Deliveries of 125 out of 149 on order had been made as this was written, to Wings F13 at Norrköping, F17 at Rønneby and F21 at Lulea, and to a squadron in F4 at Östersund. By 1987 a total of 17 squadrons will be fully equipped.

Below: Sweden is proud of the superb JA37 interceptor, which has virtually no shortcomings; this one has the gun, two RB71s and two RB24s. It can even disperse safely away from vulnerable airfields, which is what every squadron must do if it is to survive in warfare.

Saab 39 Gripen

Origin: Saab-Scania AB, Sweden.
Type: Multirole fighter.
Engine: One 18,000lb (8,165kg) thrust Volvo Flygmotor RM12 augmented turbofan (licensed variant of GE F404).
Dimensions: (Approximate) Span 26ft 3in (8.0m); length 45ft 11in (14.0m); other figures not finalized.
Weights: The only figure is 'normal max 17,645lb (8,000kg)'.
Performance: Max speed (hi) about 1,320mph (2,135km/h, Mach 2), (sea level) supersonic; required field length, well below 3,280ft (1,000m).
Armament: One 27mm Mauser BK27 gun; four wing pylons for RB71 Sky Flash AAMs, RBS15F anti-ship missiles or various other attack loads; wing-tip rails for RB24 Sidewinder AAMs; max weapon load not given.
History: First flight scheduled for 1987.
User: To be Sweden.

Fifth in the totally successful series of jet combat aircraft created by Saab, the JAS 39 actually has the maker's number 2110, the JAS 39 designation signifying Jakt (fighter), Attack, Spaning (reconnaissance). Partly because of inflation, it is the smallest of the Saab fighters, but in versatility it will be the greatest, with an all-round capability exceeding even that of the Viggen, apart from the total weight of weapons carried.

Saab has had to tread a careful path between running too high a risk and failing to create an aircraft technically advanced enough to remain competitive into the 21st century. For example, 30 per cent of the airframe will be made of high-strength composites, and British Aerospace is the chief subcontractor for the wing, which is largely of carbon-fibre construction and is provided with powered leading and trailing surfaces for maximum combat agility, the leading flaps incorporating a dogtooth. Other composite parts include the vertical tail, inlets, rear-fuselage airbrakes, nose and all gear doors.

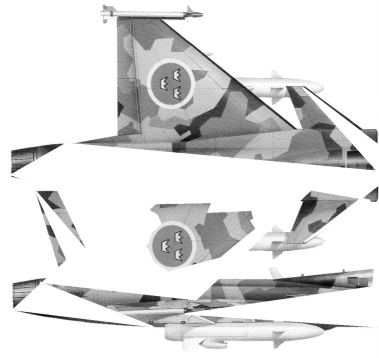

In conjunction with the fully powered, swept canard foreplanes this wing should give the Gripen (Griffon) a combat agility equalling that of any aircraft flying in 1986. Having control surfaces both ahead of and behind the centre of gravity is expected to lead to new control capabilities (such as those explored by the F-16/AFTI), with the ability to change attitude or trajectory independently. The single-wheel landing gears, designed for no-flare landings, with a braked nosewheel, confer the ability to operate safely, in the worst winter weather, from rough airstrips, highways and dirt roads. A further requirement for all Swedish military equipment is that front-line servicing be handled by short-service conscript personnel, so everything has to be reliable and foolproof.

The cockpit will of course be totally new, with a Martin-Baker S10LS seat, Hotas controls, a diffractive-optics HUD and three electronic displays, reprogrammable by the pilot to show just the items he needs at each point in the mission. Other features include fly-by-wire controls (tested in a Viggen), rear-fuselage airbrakes, plain lateral engine inlets, a Ferranti/Ericsson multimode radar and optional pod-mounted FLIR and laser ranger (which together handle the reconnaissance mission, apart from pod-mounted optical cameras), and extremely comprehensive internal and external EW systems, with a comprehensive jamming and dispensing capability.

The RM12 engine is more powerful than previous F404 versions, and among many minor changes is its reinforcement to improve resistance to bird ingestion. Fuel is housed in self-sealing main and collector tanks in the fuselage, the French company Intertechnique being responsible for the computer-controlled monitoring and distribution system. Lear Siegler supplies the triply redundant FBW flight control system, with analog back-up, the canards, leading and trailing wing flaps and rudder all being driven by Moog hydraulic power units (the leading flaps having rotary actuators). Altogether there are approximately 30 computers in the Gripen, everything being connected to a flexible data bus. Microcomputers handle such systems as flight control, air data, fuel, inertial navigation, environmental control (BAe Dynamics) and hydraulics (Abex/Dowty). Lucas Aerospace supplies the auxiliary and emergency power system, comprising a gearbox-mounted turbine, hydraulic pump and AC generator. In the emergency modes the turbine is driven either by engine bleed or APU air, or using stored, pressurized oxygen and methanol fuel. The APU is a Microturbo gas turbine, and the same company supplies the pneumatic main engine starter.

By the year 2000 it is hoped that a force of 140 Gripens can be deployed, including about 25 tandem dual-pilot versions, at an estimated cost of SKr 25 billion. The first of five prototypes was due to fly in 1987, and service is scheduled for 1992–93.

Left: Though the first prototype Gripen was fast taking shape as this book was written, no photograph had been released and in fact very little has been published on this challenging programme. Though significantly smaller, lighter and thus less horrendously expensive than other fighters for the 1990s, the Gripen is expected to be as good as any rival in a dogfight and also to have very useful capability in attack and reconnaissance missions. This artwork shows an anti-ship attack configuration, with two heavy RBS15F missiles and two tip-mounted RB24s for self-defence. It is not yet known whether these versatile aircraft will be painted in attack camouflage, as shown.

Shenyang J-6 (Farmer)

Origin: Initial design by Mikoyan/Guryevich OKB of Soviet Union; developed and produced in People's Republic of China.
Type: Tactical fighter, attack and reconnaissance aircraft.
Engines: Two Shenyang WP-6 (derived from Soviet Tumanskii R-9BF-811) afterburning turbojets each with max rating of 7,165lb (3,250kg) thrust.
Dimensions: Span 30ft 2⅓in (9.2m); length (most, inc probe) 48ft 10½in (14.9m), (JJ) 44ft 1in (13.4m); height overall 12ft 8¾in (3.88m); wing area 269.1ft² (25m²).
Weights: (Basic J-6) Empty 12,700lb (5,760kg); loaded (two tanks and two Sidewinders) 19,764lb (8,965kg), (max loaded) 22,046lb (10,000kg).
Performance: (J-6) Max speed (clean, hi) 955mph (1,540km/h, Mach 1.45), (clean, lo) 832mph (1,340km/h); max climb rate over 30,000ft (9,144m)/min; service ceiling 58,725ft (17,900m); combat radius (hi, two tanks) 426 miles (685km).
Armament: (J-6) Three Type 30-1 guns (30mm calibre), one in each wing root and one under the right side of the nose, each with 80 rounds; four wing pylons, the inners normally carrying two Sidewinders or AA-2 'Atoll' AAMs or 500lb (227kg) bombs or various rockets and the outers carrying drop tanks of up to 251gal (1,140l) size.
History: First flight (Soviet I-350M) 18 September 1953, (J-6) December 1961.
Users: Albania, Bangladesh, China, Egypt, Iran, Iraq, Kampuchea, Pakistan, Tanzania, Vietnam and (not yet confirmed) Zimbabwe.

Below: Almost discounted from the late 1950s to the late 1970s, the old MiG-19 has devastating guns and impressive flying qualities. This is a Shenyang J-6C of the Pakistan Air Force.

The first fighter in the world to be designed (in 1950–51) for supersonic speed on the level, the MiG-19 has remarkable wings swept at 53° yet fitted with large outboard ailerons as well as high-lift flaps. The circular-section fuselage widens towards the rear to accommodate two slim afterburning axial engines side by side, and the horizontal tail is of the slab type. The levered-suspension landing gears have a wide track, and a large door-type airbrake is hinged under the belly.

Good features of the basic design include an excellent flight performance and manoeuvrability and the devastating firepower of the 30mm guns, which is appreciably greater than that of Àdens or DEFAs of the same calibre. China bought a licence in 1958, calling the basic MiG-19S fighter the J-6. This entered Chinese service in mid-1962. Subsequently several thousand J-6 variants have been built, almost all of them after 1966. In addition to the basic J-6, Chinese models are the J-6A, with a limited all-weather capability; the J-6B, with the guns replaced by four K-5M (AA-1 'Alkali') AAMs; the mass-produced J-6C day fighter, with the braking parachute relocated beneath the rudder; the J-6Xin ('J-6 new'), with a Chinese interception radar in a slim needle-point radome in the centre of the nose; the JJ-6 tandem-seat dual trainer, with semi-automatic seats slightly staggered under a long, flat-topped canopy which hinges open to the right; and the JZ-6 fighter-reconnaissance aircraft, with the nose gun removed and two cameras installed between the bifurcated inlet ducts in the nose.

Very large numbers of most versions still serve with the PLA (People's Liberation Army) Air Force and Navy, and with several other air forces. Export versions are designated F-6 (the trainer being the FT-6), and among many local modifications is an underbelly fuel tank in the Pakistan Air Force (one of the biggest customers). Several users have their F-6s equipped to fire Sidewinder AAMs, and various Western manufacturers of avionics and other mission equipment have sometimes been reported to be involved in update programmes, particularly with the aircraft of the Egyptian Air Force.

Shenyang J-8B (Finback)

Origin: Shenyang Aircraft Company, People's Republic of China.
Type: Air-superiority fighter with secondary attack capability.
Engines: Two Wopen 13A-II afterburning turbojets, each with max rating of 14,550lb (6,600kg).
Dimensions: Span 30ft 8in (9.34m); length (inc nose probe) 70ft 10in (21.59m); height 17ft 9in (5.41m); wing area 454.2ft² (42.2m²).
Weights: Empty 21,649lb (9,820kg); normal loaded (fighter mission) 31,526lb (14,300kg); max 39,242lb (17,800kg).
Performance: Max speed (clean, hi altitude) 1,450mph (2,335km/h, Mach 2.2), (lo) 808mph (1,300km/h, Mach 1.06); max climb rate 39,370ft (12,000m)/min; service ceiling 65,600ft (20,000m); combat radius (mission profile not given) 497 miles (800km); max range 1,367 miles (2,200km).
Armament: One Type 23-3 gun with 200 rounds; seven pylons for PL-2B AAMs or PL-7 AAMs, or any other tactical stores up to unit weight of 1,102lb (500kg); centreline and outermost pylons plumbed for drop tanks.
History: First flight (J-8) believed 1969, (J-8 II) May 1984.
User: China, with export sales expected.

Having acquired experience with the J-7 (based upon the MiG-21F) the Chinese decided in the mid-1960s to follow the Soviet MiG design bureau and produce a 'stretched' version with twin engines. The Soviet MiG Ye-152A remained a prototype, but the Chinese J-8 I was put into limited production, an estimated 50 having been put into service with the PLA Air Force. Compared with the J-7 the J-8 I is just twice as powerful, much longer and possessed of slightly longer range. Most aspects of performance, however, were not improved, and it was generally agreed the aircraft was underpowered. It was also obvious that the operational value of the J-8 would be enhanced by the addition of a main radar.

After considerable further thought it was decided to charge the Shenyang company, which had already developed the J-6 into the Q-5 (a major redesign involving the fitting of lateral inlets), with the development of the J-8 II. At a stroke this promised to rectify two of the major shortcomings of the original J-8. The new lateral inlets and ducts not only leave the nose free for radar but also serve new engines of greater thrust. Like many Chinese engines they are based on Soviet originals, in this case the Tumanskii R-13-300. Likewise, the Type 23-3 gun is a Chinese version of the Soviet GSh-23L, and it is mounted in a recessed pack immediately aft of the nose landing gear, which closely resembles the installation of the Soviet gun in some MiG-21s. At the same time the lateral inlets, which have large splitter plates to separate the boundary layer, are similar to those of the attack versions of the MiG-23 and MiG-27, and the folding ventral fin of the J-8 II also closely resembles that of the MiG-23 family.

Lacking suitable indigenous equipment for the J-8 II, the Chinese industry managed to strike a deal with the US Department of Defense under the terms of which the People's Republic is being supplied with 50 shipsets, plus five spare kits, each comprising an AI radar, an inertial navigation system, an avionics data bus, an air data system and a HUD. These would be the main items in a major J-8 II equipment programme for the first production batch to be delivered in about 1990–91. In service, mainly on the border with the Soviet Union, the Dash-IIs will normally each carry the gun, a centreline tank, two PL-2B missiles (derived from the Sidewinder) and two PL-7 missiles (resembling the Matra Magic but allegedly with much greater range and semi-active radar guidance).

NATO has named all J-8 versions 'Finback'. No exports are permitted with the US avionics fitted, but when an exportable version appears (with Chinese or alternative Western avionics) it will be designated F-8 II.

Below: In a special paint scheme, the prototype J-8 II is seen here landing after an early flight test. Note the open air brakes.

SOKO/CNAIR IAR 93 Orao

Origin: Joint programme by CNIAR, Romania, and SOKO, Yugoslavia.
Type: Close-support, attack and reconnaissance aircraft.
Engines: Two Rolls-Royce Viper turbojets licence-built by Turbomecanica of Romania and ORAO of Yugoslavia: (development aircraft and 93A) 4,000lb (1,814kg) thrust Mk 632-41R, (production Orao and 93B) 5,000lb (2,268kg) Mk 633-47 with afterburners.
Dimensions: Span 31ft 6¾in (9.62m); length (single-seat, inc probe) 48ft 10⅔in (14.9m), (two-seat, inc probe) 52ft 2in (15.9m); height overall 14ft 7¼in (4.45m); wing area 279.86ft² (26m²).
Weights: Empty (single-seat 93A) 13,558lb (6,150kg), (93B target) 13,008lb (5,900kg); loaded (clean) (A) 19,458lb (8,826kg), (B target) 18,953lb (8,597kg); max (A) 22,765lb (10,326kg), (B target) 22,260lb (10,097kg).
Performance: Max speed at sea level (A) 665mph (1,070km/h), (B target) 721mph (1,160km/h); service ceiling (A) 34,450ft (10,500m), (B) 44,300ft (13,500m); take-off/landing over 50ft (15m) (A) 5,250ft (1,600m); mission radius (B, max external weapons, lo-lo-lo) 186 miles (300km), (lo-lo-hi) 280 miles (450km).
Armament: Two internal GSh-23L twin barrel 23mm guns each with 200 rounds; five pylons, centreline rated 1,102lb (500kg), inners 992lb (450kg) and outers 551lb (250kg), for total load of 3,307lb (1,500kg). Orao 2 can carry reconnaissance sensors.
History: First flight 31 October 1974, (B) 20 October 1983.
Users: Romania, Yugoslavia.

By far the biggest aircraft project ever undertaken in any Balkan country, the YuRom (so called from its participating countries) design crystallized as a kind of lower powered Jaguar, without great pretensions as an air-superiority fighter but capable of giving a good account of itself in front-line tactical missions in support of a land battle.

From the start the project has been split 50/50. There is no duplication, CNIAR's plant at Craiova making the forward and centre fuselage and horizontal tail and SOKO's factory at Mostar the remainder. Thus the airframe is common to both nations, and so is the Messier-Hispano-Bugatti landing gear based on that of the Jaguar, as well as the Martin-Baker 10J seats and a few other items. Yet each country has elected to go ahead with quite different systems and equipment. To the Romanians the aircraft is the CNIAR 93, while the Yugoslavs call it the SOKO Orao (Eagle).

Above: Aircraft 724 is one of the initial production batch with non-afterburning Mk 632-41R engines. It is seen carrying the standard multisensor reconnaissance pod. Some Oraos will be two-seat trainers, the second seat displacing some of the fuel.

Above: Despite many difficulties Yugoslavia and Romania have virtually completed development of the IAR-93A/Orao 1 in both single- and two-seat versions, used mainly as conversion and weapon trainers and for tactical reconnaissance. This line-up is of Yugoslav Orao 1s, including development aircraft which lack the extended wing root leading edge. Development is not quite complete on the advanced afterburning IAR-93B and Orao 2, for full combat duty.

Basic features include large slotted flaps, outboard powered ailerons, powered full-span slats, and powered rudder and slab tailplanes. Large perforated airbrakes are hinged ahead of the main gears beneath the bays occupied by the guns, which in turn are immediately below the engine inlet ducts (which are very simple). A braking parachute is housed beneath the rudder. A Lerx and a narrow strake along each side of the nose improve airflow in tight turns (7g is permissible).

The cockpit is pressurized and has an upward-opening canopy. That of the Orao would be familiar to an RAF Jaguar pilot, but the IAR 93B has a more Soviet-type avionics fit, including comprehensive EW systems. No radar has been requested.

A proportion of production machines will be two-seaters, which have dual pilot cockpits, the front cockpit moved slightly forward and the rear cockpit in place of a fuselage fuel cell giving reduced endurance. The production aircraft have integral-tank wings, replacing small separate bladder cells in aircraft flying before 1984.

It is possible that after so great a passage of time the original national requirements have changed and the Yugoslavs are keeping a low profile on this programme, though Romania has ordered 29 IAR 93As and 165 IAR 93Bs for inventory service and these are now being delivered.

Below: This side profile again shows the Yugoslav single-seat Orao in the initial non-afterburning version. The tandem-seat dual trainer versions do not have a rear ventral fin.

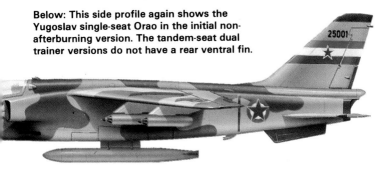

Sukhoi Su-15, 21 (Flagon)

Origin: The OKB named for Pavel O Sukhoi, Soviet Union.
Type: All-weather interceptor. Data for Su-21.
Engines: Two Lyul'ka afterburning turbojets, each rated at 22,480lb (10,197kg) thrust with full afterburner.
Dimensions: Span 34ft 6in (10.53m); length (inc probe) 68ft (20.5m); height 16ft 7in (5.05m); wing area 385ft² (35.7m²).
Weights: Empty about 22,490lb (10,200kg); loaded (clean) about 35,275lb (16,000kg), (max with external tanks) 39,990lb (18,140kg).
Performance: Max speed (clean, 36,000ft/11,000m), about 1,650mph (2,655km/h, Mach 2.5); (with AAMs) about 1,380mph (2,230km/h, Mach 2.1); initial climb rate about 45,000ft (13,700m)/min; service ceiling about 65,600ft (20,000m); combat radius (hi) about 450 miles (725km), (with tanks) 620 miles (1,000km); ferry range about 1,400 miles (2,250km).
Armament: Four wing pylons for AAMs, a typical load comprising two medium-range AAMs (AA-3 'Anab' or R-23R/AA-7 'Apex', each in both IR and radar versions) on the outer pylons and two close-range AAMs (R-60/AA-8 'Aphid') on the inners, the latter sometimes being paired to give a total of six missiles; two body pylons plumbed for drop tanks but also alternatively used to carry two GSh-23L gun pods, each with 200 rounds.
History: First flight late 1965; service delivery about 1969.
User: Soviet Union (PVO).

Via the single-engined Su-9 and -11, now no longer with PVO combat regiments, the Su-15 was developed with two smaller engines in order to provide twin-engine safety and greater thrust for higher flight, to make room for more internal fuel, and also to leave the nose free for a large radar. Like all PVO machines, it was designed to operate from long paved runways, so unlike FA aircraft it has an extremely high wing loading. This goes well with the mission of long-range stand-off interception, but eliminates good close dogfight performance and also results in take-off/landing speeds close to 300mph

Right: This 'Flagon-C' is one of the original Su-15U series, with a conical radome and pure delta wing of only 29ft 6in (9m) span and the original simpler engine air inlets. The aircraft has a natural metal finish.

(482km/h) at maximum weights. Anti-skid brakes with computer control are fitted, together with a large cruciform brake chute.

Aircraft in current service have a wing of increased span, with a midspan kink and reduced sweep outboard, which improves field length and low-speed handling. This results in the revised designation Su-21. They also have twin nosewheels, a newer radar (called 'Twin Scan' by NATO) in a curved ogival radome, and uprated engines fed by improved inlet ducts. Missiles have been updated and gun pods added. There have been two generations of dual-pilot tandem trainers. These have the NATO code name 'Flagon-C' instead of a name beginning with 'M', suggesting that the aircraft have a full combat capability.

About 750 have been in use for many years, but production ceased some time ago. The only major shortcoming of the Su-15 is that the mission radius is not great enough to cover the whole of the Soviet Union's vast frontier.

It was an Su-15 from a PVO regiment in the Far East that on 1 September 1983 shot down Korean Air Lines Flight 007, inward bound to Seoul, killing the 269 on board. Hours earlier a USAF RC-135 had been near the area, but there can have been no possible confusion over the identity of the 747.

Above: Pilots of the Voyska PVO (Air Defence Forces) cluster round the cockpit of an Su-21, whose kinky wings contrast with the pure delta shape of the original Su-15. Unlike most Soviet fighters, these all-weather interceptors need very long paved runways, but that is no handicap to an aircraft tasked with strategic defence of the homeland. Note the engine afterburner bay cooling inlets by the fin.

Left: An Su-21 'Flagon-F' with 'Anab' and 'Aphid' missiles but without the gun pods. The latter, which are carried well below the fuselage on deep pylons, confer a valued extra capability when close to targets, but take the place of drop tanks which are also desirable to extend combat radius as reported in the data above.

Sukhoi Su-17, 20, 22 (Fitter)

Origin: The OKB named for Pavel O Sukhoi, Soviet Union.
Type: Ground-attack fighter.
Engine: (Most) One Lyul'ka AL-21F-3 afterburning turbojet with ratings of 17,200/24,700lb (7,800/11,200kg); (current variants) one Tumanskii R-29B afterburning turbojet with estimated ratings of 17,635/25,350lb (8,000/11,500kg).
Dimensions: Span (28°) 45ft 11in (14.0m), (68°) 32ft 9⅓in (10.0m); length (basic 17, inc nose probes) 59ft (18.0m), (later variants) 60ft 9in (18.5m); wing area (28°) 431.6ft² (40.1m²).
Weights: (Estimated) Empty (Fitter-C) 22,050lb (10,000kg), (J) 21,715lb (9,850kg); loaded (clean) (C) 30,865lb (14,000kg), (J) 34,170lb (15,500kg); max loaded (C) 39,020lb (17,700kg), (H) 42,330lb (19,200kg).
Performance: Max speed (clean, typical, sea level) 800mph (1,290km/h, Mach 1.05), (36,000ft/11,000m) 1,380mph (2,230km/h, Mach 2.1), (sea level, typical external stores) 650mph (1,050km/h); initial climb rate (clean) 45,275ft (13,800m)/min; service ceiling 59,050ft (18,000m); take-off run ('Fitter-C') 2,035ft (620m); combat radius (C, 2,000kg bomb load, hi-lo-hi) 391 miles (630km), (H, 3,000kg bomb load, hi-lo-hi) 435 miles (700km); ferry range, four tanks (C) 1,400 miles (2,250km), (H) 1,700 miles (2,750km).
Armament: Two NR-30 guns each with 70 rounds and two K-13A ('Atoll') or R-60 ('Aphid') AAMs; eight pylons (tandem pairs under fuselage, under wing root and under wing-pivot fences) for total of 8,820lb (4,000kg) external ordnance/tanks.
History: First flight (Su-22IG) 1966, (production 17) probably 1970.
Users: (Various sub-types) Afghanistan, Algeria, Czechoslovakia, Egypt, Iraq, Libya, Peru, Poland, Soviet Union, Syria, Vietnam, Yemen Arab Rep, Yemen People's Rep.

When the Su-22IG ('IG' meaning variable geometry in Russian) was demonstrated at an air show in 1967 few Western analysts took it seriously. It was basically an Su-7 with just the outer portions of its wings pivoted. Five years later it was suddenly discovered that large numbers of slightly improved models were in service, and from 1972 until 1977 many successively upgraded examples were put into use by Soviet Frontal Aviation, AVMF (Naval Aviation) and two WP air forces. Others have been exported, notably to Peru (52 remaining in use) and Libya (102).

Below: A two-seat Su-17U 'Fitter-G' on finals, with wings fully spread, slats and flaps deployed and instructor periscope raised. These are big aircraft, roughly in the class of the F-105 Thunderchief.

**Above: This Libyan Su-22 'Fitter-J' was photographed by aircraft of
the US Navy in August 1981. It is carrying tanks and K-13A 'Atolls'.**

The perfection of this partial 'swing-wing' configuration came in Moscow
(TsAGI) in late 1963, and it was studied in connection with such machines as
the M-4, Tu-22 and Tu-28/128 (and actually put into production with the Tu-
22). Meanwhile, Sukhoi had already planned a series of improvements to the
Su-7 involving later engines, dorsal spines of increasing size (as seen on the
MiG-21), greater weapon loads and improved EW suites. The first stage was
the adoption of the big AL-21 engine which, despite its smoke at full power,
burns less fuel than the AL-7 on most missions while giving much greater
thrust.

Internal fuel was slightly increased, but the really big difference was that the
swing wing and more thrust eliminated the previous range/payload shortcomings; in round figures this initial VG version, the Su-17 series, lifts twice the
weapon load over mission radii increased by 30 per cent while eliminating ATO
rockets and yet using airstrips half as long as previously! At the same time
control input forces are reduced and in-flight agility is improved, both turn
radii and rate of roll being dramatically better.

Many of these early Su-17s are still in use, along with improved models with
a longer nose housing a laser receiver in the conical inlet centrebody and a
chin fairing which among other things accommodates a terrain-avoidance
radar. Almost all aircraft, including two-seaters (which have a down-tilted forward fuselage to improve view), have eight stores pylons. Some, including
two-seaters, have only one gun, in the right wing root.

The non-fighter designations Su-20 and 22 were applied to all subsequent
variants, the former being the export Su-17 (including aircraft for WP countries), which all have various avionics deletions compared with those in Soviet
service. Peru complained that its first batches, which have the designation
Su-22 bestowed for export purposes though they are basically simplified 17s,
were gravely lacking in navaids, had an almost useless Sirena 2 RWR and
were fitted with IFF (not the usual SRO-2M) which was incompatible with
SA-3 'Goa' SAMs supplied at almost the same time!

By this time Peru had signed for later variants, called 'Fitter-F' and 'Fitter-J'
by NATO, the latter version being a member of the final sub-family with the
smaller and much later-technology Tumanskii engine and a redesigned
fuselage and tail. Features of these aircraft include a much deeper spine providing a major increase in internal fuel, a raised and redesigned cockpit giving
a better pilot view and more room for additional avionics, two extra pylons, a
slightly bulging rear fuselage, and a vertical tail of increased height, with a dorsal fin, and an added ventral fin. In 1984 another single-seat version was iden-
tified with a ram-air inlet in the front of the extended dorsal fin. This received
the NATO name 'Fitter-K'.

Two-seaters of this family have a cockpit and canopy arrangement totally
different from earlier versions, including a small metal rear canopy with a
square window on each side. It is not known if a periscope is fitted; in earlier
two-seaters (called 'Moujik'), this can be extended at below 373mph
(600km/h).

Sukhoi Su-24 (Fencer)

Origin: The OKB named for Pavel O Sukhoi, Soviet Union.
Type: All-weather attack and reconnaissance aircraft.
Engines: Two Lyul'ka afterburning turbojets each estimated at 16,975lb
(7,000kg) dry and 24,250lb (11,000kg) thrust with max afterburners.
Dimensions: (Estimated) Span (16°) 57ft 5in (17.5m), (68°) 34ft 5½in
(10.5m); length overall 69ft 10in (21.29m); height 19ft 8¼in (6m); wing area
(16°) 500ft² (46.4m²).
Weights: (Estimated) Empty (equipped) 41,887lb (19,000kg); loaded
(clean) 64,000lb (29,000kg); max 90,390lb (41,000kg).
Performance: Max speed (clean, 36,000ft/11,000m) 1,440mph
(2,320km/h, Mach 2.18), (clean, sea level) about 870mph (1,400km/h,
Mach 1.14), (max external load, hi) about 1,000mph (1,600km/h, Mach
1.5), (max external load, sea level) about 620mph (1,000km/h, Mach 0.87);
service ceiling (with weapons) 52,500ft (16,000m); combat radius (lo-lo-lo,
17,630lb/8,000kg bomb load) 200 miles (322km), (lo-lo-hi, 5,510lb/2,500kg
bomb load) 590 miles (950km), (hi-lo-hi, 5,510lb/2,500kg bomb load) 1,115
miles (1,800km); ferry range (six tanks) about 4,000 miles (6,440km).
Armament: Eight identical MERs (multiple ejector racks) each rated at
2,205lb (1,000kg), four under fuselage, two under fixed gloves and two
pivoted to swing wings, for total load of 24,250lb (11,000kg), including
AS-7 and AS-14 missiles; glove pylons plumbed for largest drop tanks seen
on Soviet aircraft; two large blisters cover items installed in the underside
of the fuselage, one of which (and possibly both) is a gun. See text.
History: First flight believed 1969; service entry 1974.
User: Soviet Union.

Spurred by the USAF TFX (F-111) programme, this aircraft was planned at the same time as the MiG-23, and used the same excellent aerodynamics, but was fitted with two engines instead of one. Despite the fact that it is a fundamentally very old and uncompetitive engine, the consensus of Western opinion is that the Su-24 is powered by the AL-21F-3, or a close relative. This is despite the fact that the installational features familiar with this powerplant are absent.

From the start the Su-24 was a top-priority project, with nothing whatsoever compromised. Design engineers were made up into the biggest team ever seen, including many drawn from Poland's PZL, and in every detail the result is the very best that can be achieved. In many respects the Su-24 resembles the Tornado, though on a physically larger scale; it follows the F-111 in only one major feature — side-by-side seating for the pilot and weapon-systems officer. Unlike the American machine it has half its heavy weapon load under the fuselage, and the way the doors over the bays for the twin-wheel main gears fold down towards each other is particularly neat, the large panels immediately in front of them (covering the unidentified internal items) being the airbrakes.

There is no doubt that the maximum wing loading of the Su-24 is greater than that of any other combat aircraft at some 180lb/ft² (878kg/m²), and this, combined with the maximum sweep of 68° and the near-absence of a fixed portion, must result in outstandingly good, buffet-free ride qualities in low-level missions at full power. In view of the totally uncompromised nature of this aircraft it is probable that the wing has a Mach/sweep programmer which ▶

Below: Photographed over the Baltic by an aircraft of the Swedish Air Force, this Su-24 is of the model known to NATO as 'Fencer-C'. Sooty trails are common with Lyul'ka engines.

**Right: This profile artwork shows the original
Su-24 version to enter service, with the NATO
name 'Fencer-A'. Modifications since that
aircraft entered service in 1974 appear to have
been confined to additions and upgrades to
give enhanced capability.**

► continuously adjusts wing sweep, unlike the direct manual control needed on
the Su-17/20/22.

Other airframe features include fully variable engine inlets, with auxiliary
doors and ejectors; slender wings with full-span slats and double-slotted
flaps; roll control by wing spoilers (at low speeds) and powered tailerons; a
single vertical tail plus ventral fins at the chines of the wide, flat-bottomed rear
fuselage; and easily the best overall avionics fit seen on any tactical aircraft in
service anywhere. Details are still the subject of speculation, and variations
are already responsible for the identification by NATO of three in-service versions called 'Fencer-A', 'B' and 'C'.

There may be considerable internal differences between these versions, but
the external changes are fairly minor. 'Fencer-A' has a rear fuselage of roughly
rectangular section, enclosing the afterburners and nozzles with a flat side and
upper/lower structure; 'Fencer-B' has a rear fuselage more closely tailored to
follow the outer shape of the afterburners and nozzles, with a curved external
profile and a deeply dished underskin between the engines; and 'Fencer-C',
first seen in 1981, has a more complex array of sensors on the tip of the nose,
one being a pitot head at a higher level, whilst on each side just ahead of the
wing gloves are blister fairings very similar to those seen low down on the forward fuselage of the MiG-23BN 'Flogger-H', sometimes said to be CW radar il-
luminators for ground targets.

The main radar is a pulse-doppler set of remarkable power and versatility,
with a scanner diameter of at least 49in (1.25m). Terrain-following capability is
provided by secondary TFR sets as in the F-111, and a separate doppler
navigation radar is situated on the ventral centreline. The entire aircraft is

Left: Though not in colour, this is one of a series of exceptional photographs showing the new 'Fencer-C' version in the neighbourhood of an airbase. The extremely high wing-loading is obvious, and this should make for rock-steady flight at full power at low level, especially with the wings fully swept. New features include the arrays of air-data sensors on the nose and extra avionics aerials (so they are interpreted) ahead of the wing roots and on the lower flanks of the fuselage well back from the inlets. Like the Tornado (but unlike the F-111), a very heavy weapon load can be carried on pylons beneath the fuselage.

covered with avionics, most of them flush or served by very small blisters. A laser ranger and marked-target seeker is in a small chin fairing, and the tail is a forest of flush aerials and small pods or blisters, varying from one aircraft to another.

It is probable that the internal EW/ECM suite is more comprehensive than that of any other supersonic aircraft, though details are still being investigated by Western analysts. There is not the slightest doubt that the entire avionics installation was designed in parallel with the aircraft itself, and when any particular item was missing or unsuitable it was created from scratch. NATO analysts have had difficulty identifying the two ventral blisters, which cover permanently installed equipment. In the author's opinion both are guns, but of different types, in conformity with Soviet policy for use against different classes of target, but the official view is that only the left installation is a gun, the right-hand one being unidentified.

At the time of writing the number of Su-24s in service was put at 800. They are serving in all peripheral Military Districts of the Soviet Union, the main concentration being in Europe but over 200 being around China and in the Pacific coastal areas. The two giant Su-24 forces are the 4th Air Army (Hungary and the Ukraine) and the 24th Air Army (Poland), each of which has five Su-24 *polks* (regiments) with 60 inventory aircraft apiece.

According to the US DoD, some Su-24s are now being assigned to the ADD (long-range aviation) strategic force, 'and the number assigned to this task is likely to increase by 50 per cent over the next few years'. A recent traveller to Riga Airport reported seeing rows of completely unpainted Su-24s obviously in combat service.

Sukhoi Su-25 (Frogfoot)

Origin: The OKB named for Pavel O Sukhoi, Soviet Union.
Type: Close-support attack and COIN aircraft.
Engines: Two 11,243lb (5,100kg) thrust Tumanskii R-13-300 turbojets.
Dimensions: (Estimated) Span 50ft 10in (15.5m); length 47ft 6in (14.5m); height 16ft 9in (5.1m); wing area 400ft² (37.6m²).
Weights: (Estimated) Empty 22,046lb (10,000kg); loaded (forward airstrip) 36,050lb (16,350lb), (max) 41,887lb (19,000kg).
Performance: (Estimated) Max speed (clean, sea level) 546mph (880km/h); field length (forward airstrip weight) 3,300ft (1,000m); combat radius (8,820lb/4,000kg ordnance, hi-lo-lo-hi, 30min loiter) 345 miles (556km).
Armament: One twin-barrel 30mm cannon in a long chin fairing; other stores are carried on ten underwing pylons, total weight being put at 8,820lb (4,000kg).
History: First flight about 1977; service entry about 1981.
Users: Afghanistan, Czechoslovakia, Hungary, Soviet Union and (not yet confirmed) East Germany.

The Su-25's similarity to the Northrop A-9A (losing finalist in the USAF's AX competition) must be more than coincidental. The main purpose is the same: attacks on ground targets in close support of friendly ground forces, with a particular capability to take out heavy armour, fortifications and similar well-protected targets. The design is thus biased in favour of short field length, independence of ground services, good low-level manoeuvrability and a high degree of immunity to ground fire up to about 23mm calibre.

The long-span wing has anhedral, and is fitted with full-span leading-edge slats (with a dogtooth), double-slotted flaps and conventional outboard ailerons. This wing resembles that of the A-6 Intruder in many respects, not least of which is the fact that on the tips are fairings of flattened oval section which incorporate split upper and lower airbrakes which can be opened symmetrically or differentially to enhance manoeuvrability. The wing passes above the engines and fuselage tanks, and is fitted with ten pylons of which four are plumbed for drop tanks. The deep fuselage has a heavily armoured cockpit with a canopy hinged to the right and flush with the top of the fuselage downstream, thus giving a rather poor view to the rear. The large fin carries upper and lower rudders, and the dihedralled tailplane is fixed. The landing

gears have levered suspension, giving a long, 'soft' stroke, and the low-pressure tyres are suitable for rough airstrips.

There is no radar, apart from a sensitive altimeter, but the nose contains comprehensive air-data systems and a laser ranger and marked-target seeker which can be matched to precision missiles. In the tailcone is a high-capacity chaff/flare dispenser which was one of the first of its kind to be observed in action. The gun is mounted low in the left side of the forward fuselage and is of a type not previously known.

Since 1982 small numbers of Su-25s have seen much action against the Mujaheddin in Afghanistan, who have commented on its long flight endurance at low level. It has operated with heavy bombs, very large numbers (a theoretical maximum of 320) of rockets of 57mm or 80mm calibre and a powerful gun, and has often collaborated with Mi-24 'Hind-D' helicopters in making combined attacks on the same target.

Su-25s are coming off the production line at Tbilisi at the rate of about 80 per year. By late 1986 about 300 were in inventory service.

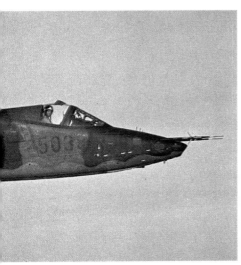

Above and left: The first good colour photographs of the Su-25 to become available were taken by Václav Juki and are of the first Czech regiment to be equipped with this specialized close-support aircraft, which flies missions similar to those of the USAF's A-10A but more closely resembles the losing A-9A. The powerful gun is of a type not previously seen. Possession by the Afghan Mujaheddin of Stinger missiles may test this tough aircraft's vulnerability.

Sukhoi Su-27 (Flanker)

Origin: The OKB named for Pavel O Sukhoi, Soviet Union.
Type: Long-range multirole and counter-air fighter.
Engines: Two augmented turbofans each in 28,000lb (12,700kg) thrust class.
Dimensions: (Estimated) Span 47ft 7in (14.5m); length (exc probe) 69ft (21.0m); height overall 19ft 8in (6.0m); wing area 690ft² (64m²).
Weights: (Estimated) Empty 33,000lb (15,000kg); internal fuel 14,330lb (6,500kg); loaded (air-to-air mission) 44,000lb (19,960kg); (max, surface attack) 77,200lb (35,000kg).
Performance: (Estimated) Max speed (hi, air-to-air mission) 1,350kt (DoD figure, converting to 1,555mph/2,500km/h, Mach 2.35); combat radius (air-to-air mission, four AA-10) 900 miles (1,450km).
Armament: Up to eight AAMs of various types including six AA-10; probably at least one internal gun; in attack role, up to 13,225lb (6,000kg) of external stores of many types can be carried.
History: First flight probably about 1976; production initiation 1983.
User: Soviet Union.

The biggest and most powerful Soviet fighter apart from the MiG-25/31, the Su-27 is based on the same aerodynamics as the MiG-29, which in any case certainly owes much to the current crop of US fighters. Compared with the MiG-29, the Su-27 is almost exactly twice as big (in area terms, i.e. a 1.4 linear scale), twice as heavy and twice as powerful. Various analyses have been published since mid-1983, the figures above being based on those issued by the US DoD in 1986; they show an aircraft significantly larger than November 1983 DoD estimates. Whether the 1983 estimates for turn rate — 17°/sec at Mach 0.9 at 15,000ft/4,572m sustained, and 23°/sec peak instantaneous value — have since been subjected to revision has not been made public, but these figures cannot be matched by the West.

Above: This artwork was prepared before the TV programme (right) showed a prototype Su-27 to the West. Apart from having the vertical tails too far forward it is broadly accurate, the vertical tails of the production aircraft being well outboard of the engines. This aircraft is bigger and more powerful than the geometrically similar MiG-29.

Despite its size, accepted in order to achieve long mission radius with many weapons, giving great persistence in air combat, the Su-27 is generally considered to be able to outfly the MiG-29, which itself was specifically designed to beat the F-14, F-15, F-16 and F-18 in close combat (and is generally accepted as being capable of doing so, the F-16 being the most difficult opponent in these circumstances). It is difficult to win by copying, and there is no question that the Soviet designers have carefully studied the US fighters before drawing the first line on paper, but with today's engines the US fighters are almost certainly unable to stay with the Su-27, which had the massive advantage of being started when the F-14 and F-15 were already flying.

The Su-27 has a completely new pulse-doppler multimode radar with the greatest possible performance against low-flying targets, and a track-while-scan capability out to a range of 150 miles (240km).

What is more serious than all the foregoing is the Su-27's armament. Not only is it now estimated — or known, because the information is published as fact — that this fighter carries eight AAMs, but they are partly or wholly of the AA-10 type. This is the first Soviet AAM which, in its radar-guided version, has its own active seeker. Thus it can be fired against a distant hostile aircraft in the desired 'fire and forget' manner, the Su-27 then either engaging other targets or turning away: there is no need to keep flying towards the enemy in order to illuminate the target with the fighter's own radar. The AA-10 flies on strapdown inertial guidance until its own active radar switches on and locks-on to the target. This capability will not arrive in Western squadrons until the AIM-120A (Amraam) becomes operational in, it is hoped, 1987–88. The Soviet AA-10 is part of the Su-27 weapon system which is already in preliminary service and was expected to be declared operational in late 1986. It includes an IR search/track system and magnifying optics.

There is probably a tandem two-seat Su-27, and a reconnaissance pod or pallet can doubtless be carried. This aircraft is reported by the DoD to be in production at Komsomolsk, in the Far East. The Su-27 is seen as possible equipment for the large new aircraft carrier being built, the first in the Soviet Navy capable of handling conventional fast jets.

Below: This TV picture shows the take-off of a prototype Su-27 (possibly the first, numbered 01). Compared with the smaller MiG-29 the nose gear is far ahead of the deep inlets (which are open during the take-off run), and the wing-root apex extension does not lie above the inlets but runs forward along the sides of the fuselage.

Vought A-7 Corsair II

Origin: LTV Aerospace and Defense Co, USA.
Type: (Except K) Attack aircraft; (K) combat trainer.
Engine: (D,H,K) One 14,250lb (6,465kg) thrust Allison TF41-1 turbofan; (E) one 15,000lb (6,804kg) TF41-2; (P) one 12,200lb (5,534kg) Pratt & Whitney TF30-408 turbofan.
Dimensions: Span 38ft 9in (11.8m); length (D,E) 46ft 1½in (14.06m), (K) 48ft 11½in (14.92m); height overall 16ft 1in (4.9m); wing area 375ft² (34.83m²).
Weights: Empty (D) 19,781lb (8,972kg), (E) 19,127lb (8,676kg); max 42,000lb (19,050kg).
Performance: Max speed (D, clean, sea level) 690mph (1,110km/h), (5,000ft/1,525m, 12 Mk 82 bombs) 646mph (1,040km/h); tactical radius (unspecified weapon load at unspecified height), 715 miles (1,151km); ferry range (internal fuel) 2,281 miles (3,671km), (max, external tanks) 2,861 miles (4,604km).
Armament: One 20mm M61A-1 gun with 1,000 rounds; up to 15,000lb (6,804kg) of tactical weapons on eight hardpoints (two on fuselage each rated 500lb/227kg, two inboard wing pylons each 2,500lb/1,134kg, four outboard wing pylons each 3,500lb/1,587kg).
History: First flight (Navy A-7A) 27 September 1965, (D) 26 September 1968, (E) 25 November 1968, (K) January 1981.
Users: Greece, Portugal, USA (AF, ANG, Navy).

One of the most cost-effective attack aircraft ever built, the US Navy's A-7 demonstrated the ability to carry such heavy loads and deliver them so accurately that in 1966 it was selected as a major USAF type, and 457 were produced of the uprated A-7D version with the TF41 engine and a new avionics suite providing for continuous solution of nav/attack problems for precision weapon delivery in all weather. This version also introduced the M61 gun and an inflight-refuelling boom receptacle.

In turn the USAF A-7D, 375 of which now equip attack units of the Air National Guard, was the basis of the A-7E, which is still a major type in the US Navy. This has a folding FR probe and if anything even more comprehensive all-weather and EW avionics than the D. The A-7 is being replaced by the F-18 but still serves with both Atlantic and Pacific Carrier Air Groups and in shore-based training squadrons.

A total of 596 of this type were delivered, of which 222 are equipped to carry the Texas Instruments FLIR pod on the inboard pylon on the right side, linked to a new Marconi raster-type HUD for an improved night attack capability. Budget limitations have held the actual supply of these pods to 110.

Above: Three A-7Ds of the 162 TFG (Arizona National Guard, since re-equipped with the F-16) photographed during tests in 1981 to decide on the most effective camouflage for use against desert and forest backgrounds. The best answer proved to be a chameleon.

The newest of all the US variants is the two-seat A-7K, 42 of which have been distributed in pairs to 11 of the 13 ANG combat-ready A-7D units plus a further 16 to the 162nd Tac Fighter Training Group at Tucson.

Greece purchased 60 A-7Hs, which are virtually A-7Es. The H equips three *mira* (squadrons), all in the maritime support and anti-ship role — 340 and 345 at Souda Bay, Crete, and 347 at Larissa in the north. The Elliniki Aeroporia also bought six two-seat TA-7Hs. Portugal had little money, and selected A-7As well-used by the US Navy and refurbished by Vought. These A-7Ps equip Esc 302 at Monte Real, tasked primarily in the strike role.

Vought has offered several attractive update programmes, including conversion to the afterburning F110 engine of 27,600lb (12,517kg) thrust. None had gone ahead as this was written.

Below: Looking highly businesslike, these A-7Es in today's low-contrast paint scheme were operating with USS *Saratoga*'s Carrier Air Wing off Libya during a period of tension in February 1986. The A-7's only disliked feature is its lethally sucking inlet.

Yakovlev Yak-38 (Forger)

Origin: The OKB of Aleksander S Yakovlev, Soviet Union.
Type: Shipboard strike fighter.
Engines: One vectored-thrust Lyulka AL-21 turbojet rated at 17,985lb (8,160kg) thrust, plus two Koliesov ZM lift turbojets each rated at 7,875lb (3,570kg).
Dimensions: (Estimated) Span 24ft 7in (7.5m); length (A) 52ft 6in (16.0m), (B) 58ft (17.68m); height overall 14ft 4in (4.37m); wing area 199.14ft² (18.5m²).
Weights: (Estimated) Empty (A) 16,200lb (7,350kg), (B) 18,000lb (8,165kg); max (both) 25,794lb (11,700kg).
Performance: (Estimated) Max speed (clean, hi) 627mph (1,009km/h, Mach 0.95), (clean, sea level) 647mph (1,041km/h, Mach 0.85); initial climb rate 14,750ft (4,500m)/min; service ceiling 39,370ft (12,000m); combat radius (max weapons, lo-lo-lo) 150 miles (240km), (hi-lo-hi) 230 miles (370km); ferry range (four tanks) 1,600 miles (2,575km).
Armament: All carried on four pylons on fixed inner wing, including GSh-23L gun pods, AA-8 'Aphid' (R-60) close-range AAMs, rocket launchers or bombs to total of 7,936lb (3,600kg), or AS-7 'Kerry' ASMs.
History: First flight probably 1971; service delivery about 1975.
User: Soviet Union.

Originally referred to as the Yak-36MP, this V/STOL shipboard aircraft is no longer being credited with level supersonic speed, but to make up for this it is much more versatile than originally thought, and carries much greater loads. The version called 'Forger-B' differs from the 'A' model in being a much longer tandem two-seater thought to be used for pilot training but possibly serving in EW and other operational roles. This version lacks the ranging radar and ordnance pylons of the single-seater.

Take-off and landing are often vertical, but rolling launches can be flown with precision guidance. The main pair of nozzles are vectored forwards up to

Below: Japanese photographer Mitsuo Shibata snapped these pristine 'Forger-As' on the deck of the _Minsk_. Lettered rings on the deck mark vertical landing spots. The span of the folded wings of this compact aircraft is only 16ft (4.88m) — very easy on deck space.

Above: This photograph was taken in 1979, again aboard *Minsk*, on that ship's first operational shake-down cruise.

10° to balance the rearward thrust of the slightly inclined tandem lift jets behind the cockpit, between the inlet ducts to the main engine. Landings are also electronically guided from the ship, such is their precision: each approach from astern is identical, at quite a low closing speed in level flight about 40ft (12m) above deck level, the final landing being vertical. Avionics are fairly limited, there being a ranging radar, radar altimeters, inertial and doppler navigation, and comprehensive IFF and electronic-warfare systems.

The aircraft's primary missions are believed to be the destruction of ocean patrol and ASW aircraft, anti-ship attack and reconnaissance. Up to 12 of these machines have been observed aboard each of the large VTOL carriers *Kiev*, *Minsk*, *Novorossisk* and *Kharkov*.

OTHER SUPER-VALUE MILITARY GUIDES IN THIS SERIES......

* Each is colourfully illustrated with hundreds of action photos and technical drawings
* Each contains concisely presented data and accurate descriptions of major international weapons
* Each represents tremendous value

If you would like further information on any of our titles please write to:
Publicity Dept. (Military Div.), Salamander Books Ltd.,
52 Bedford Row, London WC1R 4LR